Money Management

Susan M. Carlson

Money Management

ISBN: 978-1-933387-26-0

Printed in the United States of America

10 9 8 7 6 5 4 3 2 1

Quantum Scientific Publishing

Cover design by Scott Sheariss
Images courtesy of Robert Linder and the stock.xchg (http://www.sxc.hu/) website.

LINCOLN INTERACTIVE

Lincoln Interactive is dedicated to helping schools meet the demands of 21st century learners. Designing, developing, and delivering high-quality curriculum that makes innovative and effective educational experiences available anywhere, Lincoln Interactive is offering schools and communities cutting-edge strategies for creating and sustaining academic excellence.

The Lincoln curriculum is one of the first comprehensive elementary through high school series developed exclusively for online learning . This innovative, challenging, standards - based and peer - reviewed coursework is available to any school seeking to enhance and expand its educational services. Lincoln Interactive offers a full slate of both basic and advanced courses.

Lincoln Interactive is truly a 21st Century curriculum choice that provides engaging student centered educational experiences. Formatted to a unique and consistent design model, Lincoln Interactive courses offer flexibility in scheduling, a variety of course content, and regular feedback from highly trained, certified teachers. Each course provides experiences in varying learning styles. Multiple levels of interaction are available to students allowing them to receive as little assistance as they want or as much help as they need to succeed. Pod casts, streaming video, illustrations, songs, and gaming simulations create truly engaging and interactive lessons.

The Lincoln Interactive Curriculum is comprised of student friendly courses with a wide range of opportunities for academic mastery, investigation, and interaction.

Table of Contents

Money Management

UNIT 1

SECTION 1.1 - HISTORY OF MONEY

Section Objectives:

- Define the term barter.
- Define the term currency.
- Discuss the differences between bartering and a currency-based money system.

Introduction:

What do you think of when you think of **money**? It is most likely that you think of the US **currency** system with its notes (one, five, ten, twenty, fifty and one hundred dollar bills) and coins (penny, nickel, dime, quarter, half dollar, and dollar) when you think of money. Every country has its own currency. In some cases, several countries have agreed to share a currency in order to increase its influence and power in the world economy. The European Union is an example of this strategy.

Forms of money have been documented as far back as 100,000 years ago. The earliest documented form of **proto-money** is red ochre, which was used in Swaziland as a form of currency. Over time, trade beads (jewelry made of beads, shells, or ivory) became a standard tool for trade. These were the most easily divisible, transportable, and storable forms of money at the time. In order for these beads to have value, they must be scarce and difficult to **counterfeit**.

Bartering is a system of trade that involves each party involved needing what the other has to offer. A successful barter means that the people involved in the exchange both obtain what they need in trade for what they have. This usually involves significant **negotiation** between the parties to strike the best deal. This system of trade is used in cultures where no monetary system exists.

For example, let's say you are a carpenter who needs dental work done and you happen to know a dentist who needs carpentry done. The two of you could negotiate a barter, or exchange of services, that would not involve the exchange of currency. Each party would offer service in trade for service. A dental checkup might be worth

Money Matters **1**

Did you know that wooden bills were made temporarily and used in Tenino, WA, because there was a cash shortage and wood was readily available?

two hours of carpentry. Both parties get what they need and no currency is required to complete the exchange.

As you may imagine, there are difficulties maintaining a true barter system, especially when the items being bartered may be available for only part of the year (seasonally). For example, strawberries ripen in June in Wisconsin, but wheat does not ripen until late summer. The strawberries will be gone before the wheat has ripened, making it difficult for the strawberry farmer and the wheat farmer to barter directly. Another option is for the strawberry farmer to trade strawberries for an **intermediate commodity**, which can then be traded for the wheat when it ripens. Intermediate commodities can be perishable or non-perishable. Those that don't perish and are in steady demand throughout the year have been known to develop a standardized value, effectively acting as money within the community and making it easier for people to get what they need in the marketplace. Where several key goods are commonly traded, barter systems usually lead to those goods being given monetary properties. A modern example of an item being given monetary properties is the use of cigarettes in prisons as a form of currency.

> ## Money Matters 2
>
> *Did you know that the first banks were probably religious temples?*

The ancient cultures of South America used shells found near the sea to trade for goods with the tribes living in the high mountains. As the shells moved away from the sea, they gained value because they were not readily available. The people in the mountain villages would trade what they considered a fair amount of a good, for example, wool, for a specified amount of currency (or number of shells).

Standardized Coinage was developed after people discovered ways to assess the purity of precious metals, such as gold, using a tool called a **touchstone**. Touchstones required those assessing the value of the precious metal to estimate the purity

of the metal and also the total value based on weight and purity. Standardized coins were developed to allow those engaged in a trade to know the value of the coin being used. Coins were typically developed by governments to streamline trade. Coins are given specific values by the governments minting them. For example, pennies, nickels and dimes in the US currency system all have different values. A nickel has five times the value of a penny and a dime has two times the value of a nickel.

Representative money is the result of the practice of banks giving receipts for deposits of precious metals to the people making the deposit. People soon began using the receipts as a form of currency instead of the precious metal they represented. This is where the term "as good as

gold" comes from. A note that could be used to collect $5.00 of gold from the bank would also be used in direct exchange for a service or good. The US currency system used to be fully backed by gold. This is no longer the case because of the practice of fractional reserve banking, in which bankers would print receipts worth more than the actual gold or silver on deposit in the bank. Fractional reserve banking is the basis of most currency systems in the world now.

In 1971, the United States switched to **fiat money**, or money whose value is determined by the government and considered **legal tender**. Fiat money is not backed by gold like representative money is. Fiat money is often introduced by the government in times of war or when the government needs to print more money without having the gold to back it up. When the government produces money more rapidly than the economy grows, this can lead to an oversupply of money, which reduces the value of the money and can lead to inflation.

The final money concept we will discuss in this section is **credit**. Credit is typically given to a person in the form of a loan, either from the bank or through a credit card, and needs to be paid back to the institution that made the loan, usually with some amount of **interest** paid by the borrower for the use of the money. Credit can be a very powerful financial management tool, but can also lead to large amounts of debt, and ultimately, bankruptcy, if not used correctly.

Concept Reinforcement

1. List two types of money that are not official currency.

2. Describe how the barter system works.

3. Describe different types of money.

SECTION 1.2 - U.S. ECONOMY

Section Objectives:

- Define economic indicator.
- Define gross domestic product.
- Define GDP per capita.
- Discuss how personal and national economics affect one another.

Introduction:

The United States **economy** is complex. The economy includes business, individual, and government spending. A strong economy leads to better **standard of living** for the workers. A weak economy can reduce the standard of living because the currency loses buying power. It is affected by how people, businesses and the government use money. This section will teach you about some of the measures of the US economy and why they are important.

Basic Concepts:

The terms we will discuss in this section are **economic indicator** and **gross domestic product** (GDP), and **GDP per capita.**

Economic Indicator

An economic indicator is a statistic, or measure, about the economy. Economic indicators are used to understand how the economy is performing. These statistics are used to predict how the economy will behave in the future. Unemployment, new jobs, inflation, and gross domestic product are a few of the many statistics used.

Gross Domestic Product

Gross domestic product, or GDP, is a measure of the size of an economy. The formula used to calculate gross domestic product is: GDP = consumption + investment + government expenditures + (gross exports - gross imports).

Consumption: How much money is spent by people like your parents to buy food, pay bills and rent, and buy other things they need or want.

> Money Matters **5**
>
> *Did you know the per-capita person income in Pennsylvania increased from $9,353 in 1980 to $34,897 in 2005?*

6

Investment: Purchase of key pieces of equipment, buildings or tools needed to run a business. For households, an investment is most often buying a home.

Businesses buy software, buildings, machinery, and equipment in order to do their jobs. For example, a cement hauling business will buy a cement truck so the workers are able to deliver the cement to customers. Without the cement truck, the cement hauling business will not be able to do its job.

Government expenditures: Money spent by the government to buy goods and services. Examples include paying government workers and buying weapons for the military. Government expenditures do NOT include social security or unemployment payments, because the government does not get anything from the person being paid.

The final part of the GDP formula is a measure of gross imports (goods and services being bought from other countries for use in the United States) and gross exports (goods and services developed in the U.S. that are sent to other countries).

GDP per capita (per person) is a way to understand how well the economy is doing. This measures the average of how much each individual in a country contributes to the economy of that country. The formula for GDP per capita is:

Gross domestic product (GDP)/population = GDP per capita

For example, a country of 100 people has a GDP of $500,000. The formula for GDP per capita is $500,000/100=$5,000 GDP per capita.

Personal and National Economics:

As you learned earlier in this lesson, the economy has many different parts. Each part affects the overall health of the economy. Businesses help the economy when they are creating jobs, especially well paid jobs, selling the products or services they produce at a fair price, and making a profit.

> ## Money Matters 6
>
> *Did you know that there is about $500 trillion of US currency in circulation and that most of it is held by countries or companies that are not in the US?*

Individuals help the economy when they purchase goods and services, buy homes, save money, and invest for the future.

Workers earn income (money) from their jobs. This money is used to pay bills, buy things they need, save for the future, and do things they want to do, such as take a vacation. If the worker spends less than she earns, she is able to save money. If the worker spends more than she earns, she is often unable to pay her bills. People who fail to pay bills and save money often end up in financial trouble.

Governments also have income. Most income for a government is from taxes. Taxes are paid by individual people and by businesses. Taxes are also paid for different reasons. Individual income taxes are paid to support government functions. Some payroll taxes, such as social security, are paid into defined programs that may benefit the worker in the future. Property taxes are paid to local governments to pay for schools and other government services. Businesses pay taxes on profits they earn. Sales taxes are paid when a person or business buys something. This is a small sample of the taxes that are paid. People and businesses try to pay as little tax as possible. However, taxes support all of the things the government pays for.

The relationship between personal and national economics is very strong. A healthy economy creates new jobs, which then provide tax revenue to the government. It is important to keep in mind that each job created by business has a broader effect. Each person who has a job buys goods and services, which create other jobs, which make the economy grow. This is called a ripple effect. The same idea applies when jobs are lost. The loss of one job usually leads to the loss of more jobs. Loss of jobs means the economy gets smaller.

You may ask how the decisions made by an individual affect the larger economy. The national economy consists of individuals, businesses and the government. The choices made by each person, business or government combine to impact the national economy. An example from 2007-2008 is the effect of sub-prime lending on the national and international economy. Sub-prime lending means that banks loan money

Money Matters 7

Did you know that in the early 1900's, the government would accept dirty money to Washington to be cleaned? If the bills were in good condition, they would be washed, ironed, and re-circulated

to people or businesses at high risk of being unable to repay the loan. These loans have a much higher rate of **default**, or non-payment, than loans given to people are able to repay the loans.

Sometimes loans are made with an **adjustable interest rate**, which changes over time. The following example shows the impact of interest rate increases on payments for a $150,000 loan that has a 30-year repayment term.

Interest Rate	Monthly Payment	Difference	Overall Difference
5%	$805.23	--	--
6%	$899.33	$94.10	$94.10
7%	$997.95	$98.62	$192.72
8%	$1,100.65	$102.70	$295.42
9%	$1,206.93	$106.28	$401.70

Now that you understand how sub-prime loans can affect individuals, let's talk about how they affect the national and international economies. Remember that the actions of each person and business add up to affect the national economy. Businesses who buy the subprime loans from the bank lose money when the individual is unable to make payments. Those who invest in the businesses lose money. The end result of this is that the effect of the individuals not being able to pay their mortgages has had a negative effect on the international economy.

Summary:

As you have learned, personal and governmental money management practices have a big impact on each other. The health of an economy is measured in a number of ways. Economic indicators are statistics about the economy. These economic indicators are used to assess the health of the economy. Economic indicators can indicate growth in the economy. They can also indicate that the economy is getting smaller. Economic indicators are used to predict the future behavior of the economy. The choices made by individuals and institutions add up to affect the national, and even international, economies.

Concept Reinforcement

1. Define gross domestic product (GDP).

2. Define economic indicator:

3. Define GDP Per Capita:

4. Discuss how personal and national economics affect each other.

SECTION 1.3 - INTRODUCTION TO PERSONAL MONEY MANAGEMENT

Section Objectives:

- List key concepts of personal money management.
- Define net worth.
- Define asset.
- Define liability.

Introduction:

It is important for every person to understand the basic concepts of personal money management. This is true whether you are a student, a mechanic, doctor, teacher, professor, or the President of the country. Everyone is responsible for his or her own financial health. Each person has to think about money management based on his own situation. Things to think about are food, shelter, education, retirement, trips, and car purchases. There are other reasons to develop a financial plan as well, but these are some of the common reasons to save money.

> **Money Matters** **8**
>
> *Did you know that money does not grow on trees?*

Basic Concepts:

This section will introduce the basic concept of personal money management, also known as financial planning. We will discuss budgeting, expenses, debt, saving, insurance, net worth, asset, and liability.

Budget: A budget is a tool used to manage your money. The most basic concept you need to learn is that successful budget management means you spend the same or less money than you earn. A balanced budget means that what you spend is the same as what you earn. If you spend more than you earn, you will end up in **debt**.

Expenses: Expenses are the things you spend money on. There are essential expenses, which are the things you need to survive, such as food, shelter, heat, lights, health care, and clothing. Money left in your budget after your essential expenses are covered is called **discretionary income.**

Debt: To be in debt means that you owe something to a person or business. House loans (mortgages), car loans, and credit cards are some examples of different forms of debt. These debts involve repayment terms. This means that you have to pay a certain amount of money to the bank, for example, to repay the principal (amount loaned) and interest (payment for use of the principal) that have accrued (built up) over the time you have borrowed the money. Some debt is considered positive and some negative. Purchasing a home using a mortgage is often considered a positive debt because the home is expected to gain value. Ringing up a big credit card debt is considered a negative debt because the interest rates are high and the things bought with the credit card usually do not gain value. Each debt you take on adds to the expenses you need to include in your budget and reduces the amount of discretionary income available to you.

Mortgage: A mortgage is a specific type of loan used to purchase a home or other property. A mortgage typically has a long repayment term of 15 or 30 years. Some mortgage loans are set up differently, but these are the primary terms used. There are benefits to having a mortgage and owning a home. As we mentioned above, homes typically gain value, although that does depend upon the economy and the housing market in your area. The primary tax benefit of a mortgage is that the homeowner is able to use the interest paid on the mortgage loan to reduce **taxable income**, or the amount you are required to pay taxes on. This is called a **tax deduction**. The property tax paid on a home is also usually considered a tax deduction.

Saving: Saving is the act of putting money on deposit for future use, usually in an account at a bank or credit union. The money is safe and earns a small amount of interest while it is on deposit. Savings accounts are insured against loss by the US government for up to $250,000.

Insurance: Insurance is a tool used to reduce risk. For example, your parents have house insurance to protect against losses. House insurance will repay your parents for damage to your home. The losses covered are outlined in the insurance policy. It is very important to know what losses the insurance company will pay for and what losses the company will NOT pay for. Be sure to read your insurance policies so you know where you are protected from risk and where you are not protected.

Money Matters 9

Did you know that the biggest money monument is the Big Nickel, which is located in Sudbury, Ontario, Canada? It is 9 meters tall and 61 centimeters thick.

Asset: An asset is something that you own, either fully or partially. Examples of assets include homes, cars, fine jewelry, property, stocks, bonds, certain insurance policies, savings accounts, and other things of value.

Liability: A liability is something you owe. Liabilities include mortgages, car loans, credit card debt, and other debts.

Net Worth: Net worth is a measure of your assets less your liabilities. For example, if you have investments worth $100,000 and you have debts that total $40,000, your net worth is $60,000.

How do you bring all of these ideas together to manage your personal finances?
As you know, personal financial management includes a number of different concepts. It is important to understand the difference between an asset and a liability. Assets fall in the positive side of personal finance, meaning that they add to your financial stability. Liabilities can be good or bad, depending on what you have when you have paid off the debt. A liability that results in ownership of a home is usually a positive thing. A liability that does not result in you owning anything of value (for example, credit card debt) is often negative. The difference in these types of debt is whether you end up increasing your net worth by taking on liabilities.

It is important to develop a budget to help you manage your money regardless of how much money you earn. You may have seen stories in the press about celebrities, people we usually think of as having more than enough money to live, who do not manage their personal finances well. These celebrities sometimes declare bankruptcy because they cannot pay their bills.

A budget will help you understand how your income relates to your expenses. The first thing to figure out is how your income relates to what you spend. If you spend more than you earn, you need to look very closely at your spending patterns to see where you can cut spending. There are a lot of things people spend money on that are not essential to survival. Think about your typical day. How often do you buy something from a vending machine? How many meals do you eat in restaurants (including fast food)? How does the cost of the restaurant meals relate to the cost of cooking a meal at home? What other things are you spending money on that are not

> **Money Matters 10**
>
> *Did you know you could increase the bloom time of your cut flowers by adding a penny to the water in the vase?*

essential to your survival? You will be surprised at how much money you spend. Now that you understand how you are spending your money and have trained yourself to stay within your budget (earn more than you spend), it is time to think about how to save money for future use (next section). As you go through this course, keep thinking about how to balance income, expenses, savings and investments. Long term personal money management goals include saving for college, home ownership, and (gasp!) retirement.

Keep in mind that income changes over time because of promotions, raises, layoffs, etc. Expenses also change over time. Have you purchased a car? Are you going to college and need to save for tuition? Do you plan to take a trip somewhere interesting? All of these things will affect your budget. How will you deal with these changes? You should ask yourself a number of questions if your financial situation changes.

What do you do if you take on debt (a car loan, for example)? Does that debt affect your ability to save? Is the debt avoidable? Do you want to avoid the debt? What are the pros and cons of buying a new car or a used car?

Your ultimate goal: create and live by a budget that allows you to pay essential expenses, pay for loans, save for the future, and give you some discretionary income.

Concept Reinforcement

1. Discuss the importance of personal financial management.

2. Define the concepts of budget, net worth, asset, and liability.

3. What is the ultimate goal of personal financial management?

SECTION 1.4 - GOALS OF PERSONAL MONEY MANAGEMENT

Section Objectives:

- List typical goals for personal money management.

- List 3 things students should save money for.

- Discuss the difference between saving and investing.

- List the differences between simple and compound interest.

Introduction:

Now that you have learned a few things about the basic concepts of personal financial management, it is time to discuss the goals of personal money management. Each person will have his or her own goals related to money. Some people want to be rich. Some don't care. Some are very conservative and save every penny they are able to for a specific goal. Others are spendthrifts, meaning that they spend money more readily than others.

Goals of personal money management:

This section will discuss general goals for personal money management. There are many reasons to manage money well, most important of which is financial security and independence. Many people live paycheck to paycheck, also known as hand to mouth. This means that they are not able to cope with a financial crisis, such as a major car repair or a health problem that results in debt, because they do not have any financial cushion.

> **Money Matters 11**
>
> *Did you know that American Airlines saved $40,000 in 1987 by eliminating one olive from each salad served in first class?*

What are some specific goals for personal money management?

Paying bills on time.

Spending less than you earn.

Establishing and maintaining a good credit rating (future section).

Using credit cards wisely.

Saving for short-term goals (purchase of a car, for example).

Saving for college.

Saving for a home.

Saving for retirement.

Saving for something special to you (a trip, special purchase).

Saving and investing. What is the difference?

There is a basic difference between saving and investing. **Saving** money is a very safe approach to building wealth. The downside of a standard saving account at a bank or credit union is that the interest paid on your deposit is typically quite low relative to other ways of earning money, therefore takes a long time to generate wealth. The upside is that money deposited in a savings account is quite safe and will earn some amount of money over time, even though it is likely to be less than an investment that carries some risk. The money deposited in the bank is available for the bank to invest and earn money as long as it is in your account. That is how the bank is able to pay you interest.

Investments are fundamentally different from savings. The basic difference is that an investment always has some sort of risk associated with it. The Federal Deposit Insurance Corporation (FDIC) insures savings accounts for amounts up to $250,000. Investments, on the other hand, hold the promise of greater benefit, but also introduce a higher level of risk of loss. An investor must ALWAYS weigh the potential for a profit with the risk of a financial loss. The government does NOT insure investments against loss. Investments vary dramatically in the level of risk they introduce to your financial planning. Some investments provide a guaranteed stream of revenue. Bonds are a great example of this. If your grandmother gave you a $25.00 bond when you were born, she paid much less than $25 to purchase the bond, but you will be able to collect the full $25 when the bond matures. While your $25 bond was maturing, the government was using the money your grandmother used to purchase the bond to finance other activities, such as the military. Other investments are much more risky, such as buying stock in a new company.

People tend to save and invest for vehicles, trips, education, and retirement. One of the best investments a parent can make is the establishment of an education fund for his or her child. Level of education has an influence on income potential.

Interest is payment for being allowed to use money for some purpose. Interest is earned by putting money in savings accounts or other investments. Interest is paid when a person borrows money for some purpose.

Simple interest is calculated just as it sounds. The dollar amount is multiplied by the interest rate to calculate the amount of interest. If you put $100 in a savings account for a year and that savings account has a 5% interest rate, you will have $105 at the end of the year without putting any more money in the bank. If you leave the money in the bank for another year at 5% interest, you will earn another $5, bringing the total in your account to $110.

Compound interest is more complicated. Compound interest is the concept of adding accumulated interest back to the principal, so that interest is earned on principal plus interest from that moment on. The act of declaring interest to be principal is called compounding (i.e. interest is compounded).

Let's use the same example as above, but with compound interest. The dollar amount ($100), interest rate (5%) and time period (2 years) are the same.

$100 x 5% = $5 in interest after year 1.
The total in your account is now $105 (100+5).

$105 x 5% = $5.25 in interest earned after year 2.
The total in your account is now $110.25 (105 + 5.25).

Let's compare simple and compound interest over time. The example we will use here is $1,000 put in a savings account that is earning 6% interest each year.

Simple Interest				Compound Interest			
Year	Principal	Interest	Total	Year	Principal	Interest	Total
1	$1,000.00	$60.00	$1,060.00	1	$1,000.00	$60.00	$1,060.00
2	$1,000.00	$60.00	$1,120.00	2	$1,060.00	$63.60	$1,123.60
3	$1,000.00	$60.00	$1,180.00	3	$1,123.60	$67.42	$1,233.02
4	$1,000.00	$60.00	$1,240.00	4	$1,233.02	$73.98	$1,307.00
5	$1,000.00	$60.00	$1,300.00	5	$1,307.00	$78.42	$1,385.42

Look at the total column for simple interest and the total column for compound interest. What is the difference in the dollar amount in year 1, year 2, year 3, year 4, and year 5? Do you see how compound interest increases the total amount of money in your account each year?

Concept Reinforcement

1. List 5 goals of personal money management.

2. Describe the difference between saving and investing.

3. List the differences between simple and compound interest.

SECTION 1.5 - ACCOUNTS AND ON-LINE BANKING

Section Objectives:

- List the two most common types of accounts a person will use

   for money management.

- Discuss the pros and cons of on-line banking.

- List the fees that a bank might impose and how to avoid them.

Introduction:

There are many types of accounts used in day-to-day personal money management. The two most common accounts are:

Checking

Savings

Checking accounts provide easy access to the money in the account through the use of checks and debit cards. These accounts are typically used to pay bills and purchase goods and services that are needed by the household. Checking accounts sometimes pay interest if a minimum balance is maintained, but more often charge fees for various functions, such as debit card use or when the account balance is below a certain level. It is important to understand all of the fees associated with an account before you open it.

Savings accounts are tools used to earn some interest on money you do not need to use immediately. You have probably heard of the stories of people who store their money under the mattress. While this is safe unless you are robbed, you are also missing the chance to grow the money in that account. The Federal Deposit Insurance Corporation (FDIC) insures savings accounts for amounts up to $250,000 per account. Remember the discussion about interest, and how it is payment by one entity to use money owned by another. Putting your money on deposit in a savings account accomplishes two goals. The first is to have the money in a safe place that is

Money Matters 14

Did you know that piggy banks were developed from clay vessels called pyggs?

insured against loss. The second is to allow your money to grow by earning interest. Recall that interest is earned because you allow the bank to use it for other purposes. Interest is added to the amount you deposited (principal) to increase the total amount of money in your account.

On-line banking is a relatively new form of banking that has changed how banks operate. The adoption of the internet by the general public has driven this change. Banks have had to adapt quickly to providing on-line banking services. A couple of benefits of on-line banking are that the customer does not need to travel to the bank, all records are electronic (less paper), and banking can occur at any time during the day or night.

The author uses on-line banking to pay bills, monitor account balances, transfer funds between accounts, and research information about the bank I do business with. Think about how my adoption of on-line banking has changed how I interact with the bank. How often do I actually visit a bank? Does the bank need to provide as much physical infrastructure (people and buildings) for me now that I do much of my banking on-line? Does the bank still have to provide any physical locations for people to visit? In my case, the answer is that I do sometimes need to visit a bank to talk to a person.

Let's talk about the additional infrastructure a bank needs to have in place to support both on-line and in-person banking or their clients. Think about a bank you have visited. The bank has a building, people, security systems, equipment, street address, parking lot, and the other things required to run a physical location.

How does this translate to on-line banking? A secured physical location is necessary, but not for people to visit. It is required to house the computer and human resources needed to support the on-line banking. As a result, it can be anywhere because the customer does not need to go to this building. Robust on-line security is absolutely necessary for successful on-line banking to protect the privacy of the clients and the safety of their accounts. Clients must be confident that their assets will be protected during an on-line transaction. Think of all of the on-line scams to get access to bank accounts. It is important to be very careful about any email or other on-line request for access to your bank accounts. Scammers have even gone as far as sending emails that look like they are official correspondence from the bank. ALWAYS be aware of these and, if you are not sure about the validity, check with your bank directly to see if they are valid requests.

What else do you need to be aware of when engaging in on-line banking? Traditional banks offer a number of services such as direct deposit and automatic transfers of funds to savings accounts or to pay loans. On-line banking allows these activities, as well as others. One important activity is on-line bill paying. This service is offered both through specific on-line bill paying services, such as MyCheckFree, and as part of your bank's overall on-line banking program. Many businesses (utilities, credit card companies, etc.) also offer on-line billing services, including electronic bills and payment systems. The author's experience is that it is much simpler to maintain all banking in one system at my bank. Bill notices may come from various businesses, but it is much easier to track payments and deal with errors if you make payments through your bank's system.

> **Money Matters 16**
>
> *Did you know that a stack of 1 million $1 bills is 361 feet high?*

Fees

Banks charge fees on a number of different account types. Many banks offer several types of checking accounts that have different benefits that are of interest to different types of customers. For example, a student who does not have much money will be very interested in a free checking account that does not require a minimum balance. A wealthy person who is able to maintain a high balance in a checking account will be more interested in earning interest on the balance than worrying about the checking account fee that occurs when the account balance is below a certain dollar amount. Why would this be? If the person is able to maintain the minimum balance, the fee will not be incurred and interest will be earned. The money in the checking account is also readily available to the customer.

Here is a list of potential fees and how to avoid them:

Minimum Balance: Banks have various programs to allow customers to avoid minimum balance fees. It may be maintaining a minimum balance in a specific account, such as a checking account. It may be maintaining a minimum balance in a combination of accounts - i.e. maintaining a balance in a savings account is sufficient for the bank to waive the minimum balance fee on the checking account, regardless of the checking account balance. The way to avoid this is to know the policy for your bank or credit union and meet the requirements for having the fee waived.

Overdraft: This is a fee the bank charges for covering the cost of a transaction that draws more money from your account than is available. Overdraft fees typically range from $20-35 per transaction, in addition to the actual dollar amount of the transaction. The way to avoid overdraft fees is to balance your accounts on a regular basis and ensure that you pay out less than you have in your account. These fees are assessed on both check overdrafts (bounced checks) and debit card overdrafts.

Stop Payment Fees: Banks will stop payment on a check that you no longer wish to allow the recipient to cash. This is one of the highest fees a bank charges, about the same as bounced check (insufficient funds) charges. This can cost more than $30 PER check transaction for which you request stop payment service.

Service: As a result of the development of on-line banking, some institutions have begun charging service fees for teller services, which you use when you physically travel to or call the bank or credit union to make a transaction. Not all financial institutions charge this fee, so you need to know the policy of the financial institution that you use in order to avoid the fee.

Checks: Banks provide checks to their customers for a fee. There are also private services that sell checks to customers outside the banks, often at a lower cost. If you are going to use checks, you will not be able to avoid this fee, but you can elect to pay the bank rate or the private service rate for the checks themselves.

ATM: Debit cards are now a standard way to access the money in your checking and savings accounts. Financial institutions charge for this service in different ways. Some charge a flat fee for using your debit card each month regardless of the number of times you use it. Others charge a fee only after a certain number of transactions occur. Some do not charge any fee. Most institutions charge a fee to customers from other institutions to withdraw money or make an ATM transaction. You will be notified at the time you are making the transaction of the additional fee and the amount the specific charge.

Concept Reinforcement

1. List two common types of accounts used for personal money management.

2. Discuss the pros and cons of on-line banking.

3. List the fees that a bank might impose and how to avoid them.

Section **1.1**

_____

_____

_____

_____

_____

_____

_____

_____

_____

_____

_____

_____

Section **1.2**

_____

_____

_____

_____

_____

_____

_____

_____

_____

_____

_____

Section **1.3**

_____

_____

_____

_____

_____

_____

_____

_____

_____

_____

_____

Section **1.4**

_____

_____

_____

_____

_____

_____

_____

_____

_____

_____

_____

_____

_____

_____

Section **1.5**

_____

_____

_____

_____

_____

_____

_____

_____

_____

_____

_____

_____

Additional Notes

_____

_____

_____

_____

_____

_____

_____

_____

_____

_____

_____

_____

_____

_____

SECTION 1.6 - FINANCIAL INSTITUTIONS

Section Objectives:

- List key attributes of banks.
- List key attributes of credit unions.

Introduction:

There are many types of financial institutions that provide financial services to clients or members in the American money system. These institutions are usually regulated by a government agency. The common types of financial institutions are banks, credit unions, stock brokerages, asset management firms, and similar businesses. We will be focusing on the two types of institutions that you are most likely to use: banks and credit unions.

A **bank** is a financial institution that acts as a **payment agent** for its customers. The Federal Deposit Insurance Corporation (FDIC) insures bank deposits for up to $250,000 per account. Banks are also required to reinvest in their communities by providing services to people in low-income areas.

A payment agent accepts deposits and makes payments on behalf of its customers. The bank, or payment agent, is responsible for making sure the funds are collected from or paid to the right bank or person. Banks provide checking accounts that allow clients to write checks, which the bank will honor as long as the client has enough money on deposit. The bank also allows the client to deposit checks in the bank and collects the money from the bank on which the check was drawn. This is useful because this allows the customer to do business with one financial institution instead of having to travel to the bank listed on the check to collect his or her funds.

There are other payment methods that banks use for transferring money. These include **wire transfer, electronic funds transfer** and **automated teller machines** (ATM). A wire transfer is used to send money from one bank to another. This kind of transfer can also be made using cash at a business, such as Western Union, that specializes in wiring cash to another location. Electronic funds transfer is a common way of transferring money on a regular basis. This author makes charitable contributions using this method. The charity automatically receives the same dollar amount each month. This can also be used as an automatic way to pay bills or make loan payments if the dollar amount is the same each payment period. Automated teller machines, or ATMs, are machines that dispense cash. The first mechanical cash dispenser was developed in 1939 and installed in a New York City bank. This machine was not widely accepted and only used for 6 months, but the industry continued to develop the idea. Modern ATMs were developed in the late 1960s. They are now used around the world. This author was able to get cash from her bank account in Wisconsin using an ATM in Capetown, South Africa in 2005.

Another service that banks offer is loans. There are several types of loans. A few loan types are mortgages, car loans, personal loans and business loans. You are likely to apply for at least one of these loan types in your life. Remember how important it is to pay your bills on time and spend less than you earn? The reason this is important is that managing your money well will help you get loans when you need them. If you have a good history of paying bills on time, the bank will be more likely to give you a loan for a big purchase or to start a business. We will discuss loans in a later section.

> ## Money Matters 17
>
> *Did you know that a Canadian named Alphonse Desjardins was the first person to organize a credit union in North America?*

Credit unions are cooperative financial institutions. This means they are owned and controlled by the members. Everyone who has an account at a credit union is a member of the credit union. As a member, the account holder has a say in how the credit union is run. Credit unions are different than banks in one other important way. The members are able to vote on whether they want to provide deposit insurance. If they choose to do so, they have to partner with a deposit insurer, often the National Credit Union Administration, to provide that service. Credit unions offer the same services as banks, even though they may use different terms for them. For example, a savings account may be called a share account, and a checking account may be called a share draft account. Credit unions in the US generally offer higher interest rates on deposits and charge lower rates on loans.

Credit unions vary in size from small volunteer organizations with a few members to large institutions with several billion dollars in assets and a large number of members, up to several hundred thousand.

There has always been some level of tension between banks and credit unions in the U.S. The banking industry has objected to credit unions since the early 20th century, when the first credit unions were formed. This tension has continued as credit unions have gained members. In the US, credit unions have over 85 million members. This is almost half of the people in the US who have deposit accounts.

A fundamental difference between banks and credit unions is their business status. Banks are typically for profit and subject to standard business tax rules. Credit unions are non-profit organizations that are owned by their members. As a nonprofit organization, credit unions do not have to pay state and federal income tax. This gives them a big advantage over banks, which do have to pay these taxes. Another advantage credit unions have over banks is that they are not required to reinvest in their communities. Their nonprofit, member owned status means that they are already doing this because of the way they do business (people helping people).

A comparison of the deposits managed by banks and credit unions in the US is available on Wikipedia. The numbers reported on Wikipedia are from the end of 2005. The National Credit Union Administration (NCUA) insured more than $515 billion at 8,965 credit unions. The Federal Deposit Insurance Corporation (FDIC), which insures deposits in banks, insured more then $3,000 billion in deposits at 8,900 banks and related institutions. Both the NCUA and FDIC are independent agencies backed by the credit of the US government. As you can see from the deposits insured by the NCUA and FDIC, banks hold far more deposits than credit unions.

Money Matters 18

Did you know the word "bank" derives from the word "bancu?" A bancu is a desk that ancient Roman moneychangers would set up in an enclosed courtyard to convert foreign currency to the legal tender of Rome.

Concept Reinforcement

1. List key attributes of banks:

2. List key attributes of credit unions:

SECTION 1.7 - INVESTMENTS

Section Objectives:

- List the different types of investments.
- Define investment risk.
- Match investment risk with the type of investment it matches.

Introduction:

Investments are used to increase wealth. Investors use different financial tools to make money. Some investments are quite safe and others quite risky. We will discuss a number of different types of investments in this section, as well as defining investment risk and discussing how risk relates to the type of investment that should be made. A key difference between savings and investment is that the value of a savings account does not change unless money is withdrawn or interest is added, while investments can gain or lose value based on a number of variables.

Types of Investments:

Bonds: A bond is a form of debt taken on by the issuer to raise money. Bonds are sold to investors at a price less than the value of the bond with the understanding that the investor will receive the full face value of the bond after the bond matures. In essence, the investors are loaning the issuer money for a specific time period with a guaranteed return on their investment (the difference between the face value and the price the investor paid for the bond). Bonds are sold for different terms (periods of time) that are usually 10 years or longer. A couple of reasons bonds are issued are to fund building of a school by a school district and to finance government activities, such as wars, that require large amounts of money. Ask your grandparents if they remember war bonds. Bonds tend to be low risk, but it is important to understand what you are investing in before making that assessment.

Stocks: A unit of ownership within a company. A stock is also known as a share. The more shares of a stock you own, the more of the company you own. The shares (common stocks) usually give the owner voting rights in the company based on the number of shares. The more shares someone owns, the greater the influence of the

Money Matters 19

Did you know that the Philadelphia Stock exchange was established in 1790?

vote. There are some types of stocks that do not include voting rights. These are called preferred stocks. Owners of these shares are guaranteed a certain level of **dividends** before any payments can be made to the owners of the common stocks. Stocks are traded on the **stock market.** The New York Stock Exchange (NYSE) is a famous example. The NYSE is a place where stock traders can buy and sell stocks based on how the stock market is behaving. You have probably heard of the Dow Jones Industrial Average or the NASDAQ. These are different measures of stock performance that are used by the stock traders to figure out how many shares of which stocks they want to buy or sell. The risk of investing in stocks depends on the type of company you invest in. For example, a well-established "blue chip" company stock is likely to carry less risk than a stock from a young, growing company in a technology field or a company in a country with unstable politics.

Certificate of Deposit: Certificates of deposit, or CDs, are similar to savings accounts in that they have virtually no risk associated with them. The difference is that CDs require that the funds be on deposit for a specified amount of time, ranging from 3 months to 5 years. Interest earned on certificates of deposit is higher than on standard savings accounts. Generally the longer the term of deposit, the higher the interest rate earned. However, this is not always the case. Be sure to investigate the specific terms of the account when opening it. A mature CD is valued at the original deposit plus interest earned. Withdrawal of funds from a CD before it is mature results in financial penalties.

Life Insurance: Life insurance is a contract between the insurance company and the policyholder. The policyholder agrees to pay a certain amount of money (a premium) at regular intervals in exchange for the life insurance company agreeing to pay a certain amount of money upon the death of the policyholder. There are two types of life insurance: term and whole life. Term life insurance provides coverage for the term, or period, that the insurance is in effect. Term life insurance does not gain value over time and the benefit to the policyholder goes away when the term of the policy expires, usually when the policyholder stops paying the premium. Whole life insurance is different from term life insurance in a couple of significant ways. Whole life insurance remains in effect for the life of the policyholder if the premium has

Money Matters 20
Did you know that the largest bond on one piece of paper was issued by the New York Cable Railway in 1884? It measures about 2 feet by 3 feet.

been fully paid. This can be done either as a one-time payment or a series of payments over time. Once the policy is paid up, the policyholder is insured until death. The second significant difference is that whole life insurance has value as an asset. People who have whole life insurance policies are able to borrow against the value of the policy if they need to. This is not possible with term insurance. Life insurance is a low risk investment.

Real Estate: The American dream has long been to own a home, or real estate. Real estate is property and buildings. Real estate tends to gain value over time, which is appealing to investors. A family invests in a home for a couple of reasons: to have a place to live and to build assets that they can use later if they need to. Real estate is typically a low risk investment. This can change, however, if real estate values are inflated and the market crashes.

Precious Metals: Most people do not invest in precious metals, such as gold or platinum, on a large scale. However, many people "invest" in things like jewelry and coin collections. These investments are only investments if the person is willing to sell them. So, for those who collect jewelry, coins, or other forms of precious metals, it is important to differentiate between having them as a collection for personal enjoyment and using them as an investment. Precious metals are typically a low risk investment, but this depends upon the price at which the investor purchased the metals. It is better to buy them at a low price than a high price.

Investment risk: There are a number of types of investment risk. The level of investment risk depends upon the type of investment. Some examples of investment risk are below.

Currency risk occurs when an investment is in a different currency than your own. For example, if you invest US$1,000 in Icelandic Kroner (ISK), there is a risk that the value of your $1,000 will vary based only on changes in the exchange rate between the US dollar and the Icelandic Kroner. This risk is independent of any risk incurred by the actual investment itself.

Liquidity risk is based on the ability of the investor to access the money invested.

If an investment is liquid, or easily salable, the risk is low. If the investment is not liquid, it will take more time to gain access to the money.

Financial risk depends upon the financial well being of the investment (company, fund, etc.). Enron is a good example of this. Financial risk was incurred because of accounting **fraud**. As a result of this fraud and the resulting investigations, the employees were unable to sell their shares of stock because of a freeze (prohibition) on stock liquidation.

Market risk reflects the effect of supply and demand on share prices on the open market. As demand increases, stock prices tend to increase. As demand decreases, stock prices tend to decrease, which can lead to financial losses. This principal applies to real estate, stocks, mutual funds, and bonds.

You have learned about most common types of investments made by individuals, as well as the risk of those investments. You have also learned about different levels and types of risk associated with investments. This knowledge will help you make informed financial decisions as you go through life.

Concept Reinforcement

1. List the different types of investments.

2. Define investment risk.

SECTION 1.8 - INVESTMENT STRATEGY

Section Objectives:

- Discuss the differences between short and long term investing.
- Discuss investment strategies.
- List the two primary goals of socially responsible investing.
- List 5 goals for financial planning.

Introduction:

The investment strategy you use to build wealth is based upon a number of factors, one of which is whether you are making a long or short-term investment. Short-term investments are used for purchases that will be made in a relatively short amount of time. An example is investing so you are able make the down payment on a car or home. People typically invest over the long-term to educate their children or pay for retirement.

Investment Strategies: Everyone has individual financial goals. Short-and long -term investments can be used to meet those goals. There are a number of investment types that can be used to meet both long and short-term investment goals. Examples of financial goals include purchase of a vehicle, home, or investment property, as well as investing in education and retirement funds.

Mutual Funds are collections of investments that are managed by professioals called fund managers. The investment types include stocks, bonds, short-term **money markets** (cash), and other **securities**, all of which carry different levels of risk to the investor. Stock funds may focus on a particular industry (energy or biotechnology, for example). Bond funds (mutual funds consisting mostly of bond investments) can vary in risk from low to high, depending upon the type of bond, the issuer of the bond, and the term of the bond. The job of the fund manager is to trade the compo-nents of the fund to realize a gain (make a profit) for the investor based on the goals of the particular fund. Mutual funds are designed to meet the risk tolerance of the investor. There are hundreds or thousands of mutual funds to choose from, all with different levels of risk.

> **Money Matters 22**
>
> *Did you know there are about 14,000 mutual funds, but only about 7,000 stocks?*

Pension Fund: A pension fund is a pool of assets used to fund the pension (retirement) benefits for an organization or group or organizations. Pension funds may ONLY be used to pay the retirement benefits of the people within the group. Pension funds invest in other financial instruments to increase the value of the fund assets. A pension fund manager is like a mutual fund manager. The pension fund manager selects different investments and manages those investments for the benefit of the fund. Most fund managers will make investments that vary highly in risk.

What kind of money do I invest?

There are two types of money that a person uses to fund investments: pre-tax and post-tax income.

Post tax investment: Post-tax money is the money left in your paycheck after all taxes have been deducted. This is also known as net income. Most investments are funded using post-tax income, including mutual funds, money markets, real estate, individual retirement accounts and Roth IRAs. Money invested in accounts post-tax incurs tax on the gain either at the end of the tax year (mutual funds, CDs, money markets and other non-retirement investments), or when it is withdrawn for use in retirement, usually at age 59 ½ or older. For example, if you invest $1,000 over a year at 10% interest, you will end up with $1,100. If you withdraw the money, you will pay tax on the $100 gain. Assume an income tax rate of 15%. You will pay $15 in tax, which reduces your gain to $85 ($100 - $15). Roth IRAs are the exception to this rule. We will discuss them in a future section.

Pre tax investment: Pre-tax investment is an important tool for long term financial planning. Many businesses offer employees the opportunity to invest in pre-tax retirement plans. The two primary account types are 401K (for-profit business) and 403B (non-profit organization). Pre-tax investments are made from your gross income, which is your income before taxes are paid. The two benefits to this type of investment are 1) that you are able to purchase more with pre-tax than post-tax dollars, and 2) the pre-tax investment reduces your taxable income, which reduces the amount of income tax you must pay. Let's say that your income tax bracket is 15%. If you designate $100 dollars a month to a pre-tax investment, the actual effect on your net income is $85 ($100 pre-tax investment - $15 in tax you do not pay) less rather than $100 less. Do you see how this can make a difference over time?

Another thing to think about with pre-tax investment is the tax burden (what you will owe in taxes) when you are able to withdraw the money. If you invest in a standard 401K or 403B, you invest with pre-tax dollars and incur a tax liability on the gains (interest over time). There are certain post-tax retirement investment vehicles that do not incur the tax liability on the gains.

Socially responsible investing is becoming more widely practiced. People who invest in socially responsible funds are concerned with both financial gain and doing social good. This means that the investment considers the environmental responsibility, workplace diversity and product safety programs of the company. Socially responsible investors also typically avoid investing in companies that profit from alcohol, gambling, tobacco, weapons, and military tools. Investors may also avoid companies that have taken a stance on abortion. People who invest in socially responsible funds are concerned with both profit and social good. They are not going to fully sacrifice one for the other, so need to find a balance that fits with their individual beliefs.

Financial planning is something we all need to engage in, both short and long-term. As a reminder, short-term investment is used to earn money to make a purchase, such as a down payment on a vehicle or home. The most common long-term investment strategy is to pay for retirement. There are investment tools that take advantage of both pre- and post-tax income. These will be explored more fully in future sections.

Money Matters 24

Did you know it cost $2.65 million to join the New York Stock Exchange in 1999?

Concept Reinforcement

1. Discuss the differences between short and long term investing.

2. Discuss investment strategies.

3. List the two primary goals of socially responsible investing.

4. List 5 goals for financial planning.

SECTION 1.9 - IMPORTANCE OF SAVING

Section Objectives:

- State the recommended percent of income that an individual should save each paycheck.
- Discuss how starting a savings program at a young age affects retirement savings.

Introduction:

You have probably heard the sayings "a penny saved is a penny earned" and "save for a rainy day." The concept we will discuss in this section is the importance of saving money and the recommended percent of your income that you should save. We will also discuss the impact of beginning a savings program at different ages.

Saving:

As you have learned in previous sections, there are a number of ways to save money and a number of reasons to do so. The general rule of thumb is that you save 10% of your income starting at a young age, you will put yourself in a healthy financial situation.

One concept that you need to understand is the **time value of money**. You may assume that one dollar today will have the same value 1, 5, or 10 years in the future. The bill itself will look the same, but you can do more with a dollar today than you will be able to do in a year. For example, if you deposit $10 (present value) in a savings account today at 5% interest. You will have $10.05 (future value) in a year. If you deposit that same $10 in a year, you will have only $10 and will have lost the chance to earn interest on it.

So, how do you figure out the future value of money? The variables you need to include in the equation are the amount invested, the time period, and the interest rate. For our example, we will use a $1,000 investment with a 7% return (interest rate).

The formula is:

Future Value = (amount invested x interest rate) + amount invested

Our example: ($1,000 x .07) + 1,000 = $1,070

This formula can be simplified. The addition of 1 (100%) plus .07 (7%) replaces adding the $1,000 back in after the interest is calculated.

Future Value = amount invested x (1+ interest rate)

Our example: $1,000 x (1 + .07) = $1,070
This can also be written as: $1,000 x 1.07 = $1,070.

The example we have used so far reflects investment for one year. Remember that investments and savings accounts often accrue on a compound basis. So, we need to figure out how to calculate the interest earned over multiple years.

Using the equation above, we will calculate interest for years 2 through 5. The dollar amount we will use is $1,070, which is the total after interest from year 1 and we will use the same interest rate of 7%.

Year 2: $1,070.00 x 1.07 = $1,144.90

Year 3: $1,144.90 x 1.07 = $1,225.04

Year 4: $1,225.04 x 1.07 = $1,310.80

Year 5: $1,310.80 x 1.07 = $1,402.55

Do you see how leaving money in an account over years increases the value of the account even though you do not deposit any more money yourself? Let's take this concept to the next step, which is long-term investment. You are now a teenager, so you have five or more decades of time in front of you to earn money before you decide to retire. What do you think will happen if you deposit $100 at age 15 and allow it to accumulate interest at 7% until retirement age (65 years old)? Look at the table below to figure this out.

> **Money Matters** 26
>
> *Did you know that the Baby Bond certificate is called a baby bond, in part, because it measures 3 inches by 5 inches in size?*

Periods	1%	2%	3%	4%	5%	6%	7%
1	1.0100	1.0200	1.0300	1.0400	1.0500	1.0600	1.0700
2	1.0201	1.0404	1.0609	1.0816	1.1025	1.1236	1.1449
3	1.0303	1.0612	1.0927	1.1249	1.1576	1.1910	1.2250
4	1.0406	1.0824	1.1255	1.1699	1.2155	1.2625	1.3108
5	1.0510	1.1041	1.1593	1.2167	1.2763	1.3382	1.4026
6	1.0615	1.1262	1.1941	1.2653	1.3401	1.4185	1.5007
7	1.0721	1.1487	1.2299	1.3159	1.4071	1.5036	1.6058
8	1.0829	1.1717	1.2668	1.3686	1.4775	1.5938	1.7182
9	1.0937	1.1951	1.3048	1.4233	1.5513	1.6895	1.8385
10	1.1046	1.2190	1.3439	1.4802	1.6289	1.7908	1.9672
11	1.1157	1.2434	1.3842	1.5395	1.7103	1.8983	2.1049
12	1.1268	1.2682	1.4258	1.6010	1.7959	2.0122	2.2522
13	1.1381	1.2936	1.4685	1.6651	1.8856	2.1329	2.4098
14	1.1495	1.3195	1.5126	1.7317	1.9799	2.2609	2.5785
15	1.1610	1.3459	1.5580	1.8009	2.0789	2.3966	2.7590
16	1.1726	1.3728	1.6047	1.8730	2.1829	2.5404	2.9522
17	1.1843	1.4002	1.6528	1.9479	2.2920	2.6928	3.1588
18	1.1961	1.4282	1.7024	2.0258	2.4066	2.8543	3.3799
19	1.2081	1.4568	1.7535	2.1068	2.5270	3.0256	3.6165
20	1.2202	1.4859	1.8061	2.1911	2.6533	3.2071	3.8697
21	1.2324	1.5157	1.8603	2.2788	2.7860	3.3996	4.1406
22	1.2447	1.5460	1.9161	2.3699	2.9253	3.6035	4.4304
23	1.2572	1.5769	1.9736	2.4647	3.0715	3.8197	4.7405
24	1.2697	1.6084	2.0328	2.5633	3.2251	4.0489	5.0724
25	1.2824	1.6406	2.0938	2.6658	3.3864	4.2919	5.4274
26	1.2953	1.6734	2.1566	2.7725	3.5557	4.5494	5.8074
27	1.3082	1.7069	2.2213	2.8834	3.7335	4.8223	6.2139
28	1.3213	1.7410	2.2879	2.9987	3.9201	5.1117	6.6488
29	1.3345	1.7758	2.3566	3.1187	4.1161	5.4184	7.1143
30	1.3478	1.8114	2.4273	3.2434	4.3219	5.7435	7.6123
31	1.3613	1.8476	2.5001	3.3731	4.5380	6.0881	8.1451
32	1.3749	1.8845	2.5751	3.5081	4.7649	6.4534	8.7153
33	1.3887	1.9222	2.6523	3.6484	5.0032	6.8406	9.3253
34	1.4026	1.9607	2.7319	3.7943	5.2533	7.2510	9.9781
35	1.4166	1.9999	2.8139	3.9461	5.5160	7.6861	10.6766
36	1.4308	2.0399	2.8983	4.1039	5.7918	8.1473	11.4239
37	1.4451	2.0807	2.9852	4.2681	6.0814	8.6361	12.2236
38	1.4595	2.1223	3.0748	4.4388	6.3855	9.1543	13.0793
39	1.4741	2.1647	3.1670	4.6164	6.7048	9.7035	13.9948
40	1.4889	2.2080	3.2620	4.8010	7.0400	10.2857	14.9745
41	1.5038	2.2522	3.3599	4.9931	7.3920	10.9029	16.0227
42	1.5188	2.2972	3.4607	5.1928	7.7616	11.5570	17.1443
43	1.5340	2.3432	3.5645	5.4005	8.1497	12.2505	18.3444
44	1.5493	2.3901	3.6715	5.6165	8.5572	12.9855	19.6285
45	1.5648	2.4379	3.7816	5.8412	8.9850	13.7646	21.0025
46	1.5805	2.4866	3.8950	6.0748	9.4343	14.5905	22.4726
47	1.5963	2.5363	4.0119	6.3178	9.9060	15.4659	24.0457
48	1.6122	2.5871	4.1323	6.5705	10.4013	16.3939	25.7289
49	1.6283	2.6388	4.2562	6.8333	10.9213	17.3775	27.5299
50	1.6446	2.6916	4.3839	7.1067	11.4674	18.4302	29.4570

The way to figure this out is to subtract your current age (15) from the future age (65). The difference is 50 years, which is the amount of time your $100 will accrue interest. The table has several columns with headers that show the percentage rate (1% to 7%). The rows represent the years. Find the point on the table where the years and percent interest intersect. The value you see there is 29.4570. If you multiply your initial deposit ($100) times the value from the table (29.4570) you will have $2,945.70 in that account without adding any more principal. Do this calculation with deposits of $1,000 and $10,000. A deposit of $1,000 will result in $29,457 in the account. A deposit of $10,000 will result in $294,570.

Let's do the same calculation starting the savings program at different ages. We will use the same interest rate and beginning investment amounts.

Starting age	20	30	40	50	60
Time invested	45 years	35 years	25 years	15 years	5 years
Multiplier from table	21.0025	10.6766	5.4274	2.7590	1.4026
$100.00	$2,100.25	$1,067.66	$542.74	$275.90	$140.26
$1,000.00	$21,002.50	$10,676.60	$5,427.40	$2,759.00	$1,402.60
$10,000.00	$210,025.00	$106,766.00	$54,274.00	$27,590.00	$14,026.00

Do you see the value of starting a savings program at a young age? This example represents only 1 deposit at different ages. How do you think the final totals would change if you continued to add money to the principal?

Concept Reinforcement

1. State the recommended percent of income that an individual should save each paycheck.

2. Discuss how starting a savings program at a young age affects retirement savings.

SECTION 1.10 - INTRODUCTION TO PERSONAL BUDGETING

Section Objectives:

- List the basic principles in personal budgeting (overview of concept).
- Discuss allocation percentages as they apply to personal budgeting.

Introduction:

We have been discussing the importance of investing and saving. The next very important concept for successful personal money management is budgeting. A personal budget is defined as a finance plan that allocates future personal income toward expenses, savings and debt repayment and will help you manage your money to meet all of your financial needs and goals.

Concepts of Personal Budgeting

Purpose: Each budget should have a goal that can be met within a given time frame. For example, a monthly budget should reflect all of the financial activities that occur in a month.

Simplicity: The KISS principle (Keep It Simple Stupid) can be applied to budgeting. Break the budget down as much as you need to without making it too complicated. The simpler the budget is, while allowing you to meet your goals, the more likely you are to keep up with it. For example, lumping expenses into categories such as food, utilities, car, entertainment, and housing will help you understand how much of your income is being used to pay for different types of expenses.

Flexibility: Budgets should be flexible. Life brings changes that will require changes in the budget. Ideally, you should review your budget on a monthly basis. Things to consider in a budget review are upcoming one-time expenses, changes in utility costs over the year, overruns in a budget category, or new long-term expenses that need to fit into the existing budget plan. For example, if you live in a place with four distinct seasons, you will need to estimate the cost of your heating or cooling bill in different seasons. If you add another person to the household, you need to budget for the things that person will need (food, clothes, housing, etc.).

Money Matters 27

Did you know that the word budget is derived from the French word bougette, which means a little bag?

It is important to be very careful of "budget busting." Budget busting means that you spend more than you budgeted. If you do this on a regular basis and are unable to get your budget back in balance, you will end up in financial trouble.

Budgeting for Irregular Income:

Many families have jobs that provide irregular income. A prime example of this is a seasonal job, such as harvesting crops, where the work is only available for a limited time each year. When a family is in this position, it is important to plan for the changes in income over time. The two keys to successful budget planning when you are dealing with irregular income is to plan a budget that reflects the average income and developing a safety cushion that can be used if the income changes are different than anticipated. A safety cushion can be developed slowly over time if the family is able to save 5-10% of their monthly income (i.e. spend 5-10% less than they earn).

Allocation guidelines:

There are several guidelines for allocating money when preparing a budget. One of the biggest considerations is your past spending pattern. In order to understand these patterns, you will have to keep track of what you spend over a month or two. It is important to track expenses using the receipts you get when you make a purchase. Estimating expenses based on memory is unreliable and will result in a budget that does not reflect reality.

Richard Jenkins, MSN Money's editor-in-chief, developed a budgeting system called the **60% Solution**. This system divides your gross income into 60%, which is spent on fixed expenses. Fixed expenses include federal, state, and social security taxes, regular bills, and living expenses, and insurance. Regular bills and living expenses include food, clothing, house payments, utilities, and car payments. The remaining 40% of the gross income is allocated across four different budget categories, including retirement, long-term savings, irregular expenses, and fun money. Jenkins recommends that the remaining 40% be split evenly between the following four categories. The exception to this is if the person has a large non-mortgage debt load that needs to be paid off. In that situation, he recommends using the funds allocated to retirement and long-term savings be used to pay off the debt. Once the debt is paid off, it is important to start putting money in retirement and long-term savings again.

Money Matters 28

Did you know that wooden bills were made temporarily and used in Tenino, WA, because there was a cash shortage and wood was readily available?

Retirement: This is money invested in a retirement account.

Long-Term Savings: Money invested for a major purchase, such as a vehicle, house renovation, education or paying off major debt.

Irregular Expenses: These are expenses that occur occasionally and are not necessarily planned for. A planned irregular expense would be a vacation or the planned replacement of an appliance. An irregular expense would be a major car repair, an unexpected medical bill, or a major house repair.

Fun Money: Money set aside for entertainment purposes, such as eating out or going to a movie.

Housing is one of the biggest expenses in the budget. Experts recommend that housing expenses (rent or mortgage) should be limited to 25% of your net income. If your net income in a month is $2,000, this means that you should spend no more than $500 on rent or mortgage. If your net monthly income is $5,000, you will be able to allocate $1,250 per month to housing. You can see how your income impacts what you can afford to pay for housing. There are some situations in which you may not be able to follow the 25% allocation guideline for housing. There are some housing markets that are very expensive, making it impossible to follow the 25% rule. If you live in an area like this, you will need to reduce your expenses in the other budget categories.

Remember that developing a budget is only the first part of the budget process. Once you have developed a budget, you will need to follow it and review it regularly to make sure you are living within your means and meeting your financial goals.

Concept Reinforcement

1. List the basic principles in personal budgeting (overview of concept).

2. Discuss allocation percentages as they apply to personal budgeting..

Section **1.6**

Section **1.7**

Section **1.8**

Section **1.9**

Section **1.10**

Additional Notes

Money Management

UNIT 2

SECTION 2.1 - EDUCATION AND EARNING POTENTIAL

Section Objectives:

• Discuss how educational level affects earning potential.

• List costs and benefits of advanced education.

• Discuss whether there is a point of diminishing returns in education.

Introduction:

I am sure that some of you who are reading this chapter wonder why it is important for you to stay in school. First - you are required by law to attend school. Second - your parents want you to learn and be successful.

There are several levels of education you can achieve: high school, technical school, bachelor's degree, master's degree, and doctorate. There are people with no degrees and people with several degrees.

The first level of education you need to achieve is to get your high school diploma. This is the absolute basic level of education you need to function in the current economy. A high school diploma means that you have completed school through grade 12. If you do not graduate from high school, you have the option of taking tests to get your GED (general educational development) certification, which means you have completed the requirements for a high school diploma even though you did not officially graduate. Regardless of which way you get the certification, you must have this level of education for many jobs, including serving in the military. This level of education is linked to the lowest income potential.

Once you have graduated from high school, it is time to decide what further education you wish to pursue. In order to decide, you need to know what interests you in a career. For some people, the best track to take is to pursue an associate's degree in a specialized technical field, such as medical imaging, cosmetology, auto mechanic, and biotechnology. Technical schools offer highly focused degree programs to students who want to complete their training in a short time and get into the work place. Most technical school programs are two years long. The degree awarded is an associate's degree. An associate's degree can lead to a well-paying job. The degree holder may run into some difficulty with promotions to non-technical jobs in the field, such as supervisors or managers.

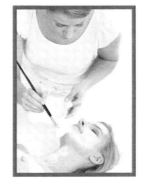

If you want to pursue a broader education, you will need to go to college. Universities and colleges offer baccalaureate degrees to those who complete the requirements. One can typically get a Bachelor of Science (B.S.) degree or a Bachelor of Arts (B.A.) degree. There are other baccalaureate degrees, but these are the two most common.

A bachelor's degree program typically has a set of **core requirements** that include the basic courses for the discipline (major) the student has selected, as well as some **liberal arts** courses. Liberal arts are broadly defined as classical education and include literature, languages, art, science, theology, math and history. These courses give the student a broad range of education in addition to the specialized courses they take to fulfill the requirements for their major. Requirements for a specific major will also include **elective** courses related to the major. Students are given a number of course options to choose from (which they elect to take) to meet their degree requirements. This gives students a chance to focus on specific topics they are interested in within the broader degree program. People with a bachelor's degree have the choice

Money Matters 30

Did you know that the estimated lifetime earnings, in 1999 dollars, for people with professional degrees are $4,400,000?

of going directly into the work force or pursuing an advanced degree. Certain disciplines are worth more in the market than others. For example, an engineering degree generally demands a higher salary than a language degree. This is not always the case. The more important thing is to pursue a career that is interesting to you and takes advantage of your skills and abilities.

Advanced degrees include masters and doctoral degrees. Masters degrees generally require an additional two years of advanced education. Common masters degrees are Master of Business Administration (M.B.A.), Master of Science (M.S.), and Master of Arts (M.A.). Again, the market determines the monetary value of the expertise gained with a master's degree. Sometimes it helps increase earning power. Sometimes it does not.

Money Matters 31

Did you know that the estimated lifetime earnings, in 1999 dollars, for people who have high school diplomas are $1,200,000?

There are many types of doctoral degrees. A few include Medical Doctor (M.D.), Doctor of Dental Science (D.D.S.), Doctor of Jurisprudence (J.D.), Doctor of Veterinary Medicine (D.V.M.), Doctor of Philosophy (Ph.D.), Doctor of Education (Ed.D.). There are many others, but we will not list them here. There are differences between the various doctoral degrees. There are professional degrees (M.D., J.D., D..D.S., D.V.M., Ed.D.) and academic degrees (Ph.D.). A professional degree typically provides a highly specialized service, such as medical care or law services. Academic degrees train the degree holders to conduct research and teach courses. A person can earn a Ph.D. in any discipline from art to zoology. Professional degree holders tend to be more highly paid than those with academic degrees. This is not always the case, however. There are professors who have made important discoveries during their research that resulted in a successful product that makes the inventors rich.

There are even people who get two or more advanced degrees. Some combinations are J.D./M.B.A. (law and business); M.D./Ph.D. (medicine and science); J.D./Ph.D. (law and science); and D.V.M./Ph.D. (veterinary medicine and science). People who achieve this level of education usually fare well financially, but may not fare as well financially as others who have less focused training.

Costs and Benefits of Education

As you may imagine, pursuing higher education (associate's degree and higher) requires both time and money. The more education you pursue, the more effort you will put into it and the more money it will take to achieve it. The good news is that there is a financial benefit to pursuing education beyond high school even when money and time are taken into account.

Education pays in higher earnings and lower unemployment rates

Unemployment rate in 2006 (Percent)	Education attained	Median weekly earnings in 2006 (Dollars)
1.4	Doctoral degree	$1,441
1.1	Professional degree	1,474
1.7	Master's degree	1,140
2.3	Bachelor's degree	962
3.0	Associate degree	721
3.9	Some college, no degree	674
4.3	High-school graduate	595
6.8	Less than a high school diploma	419

Note: Data are 2006 annual averages for persons age 25 and over. Earnings are for full-time wage and salary workers.
Source: Bureau of Labor Statistics, Current Population Survey.

Concept Reinforcement

1. How does educational level affect earning potential?

2. List costs and benefits of advanced education.

3. Discuss whether there is a point of diminishing returns in education.

SECTION 2.2 - EARNING MONEY

Section Objectives:

- List ways people earn money.

- List how these ways of earning money differ.

Introduction:

Think about the people you know who earn money. Are all of them working at a job? Are some of them self-employed? How many work full time? Part-time? Do any of them have more than one job? Are some retired? Are some independently wealthy? Is it a mystery how some people pay their bills? There are many ways people bring in money to support their lifestyles.

Ways to earn money:

Most people earn money by getting a job. Jobs have a lot of different characteristics.

Full time jobs typically require 40 hours per week of work on the part of the employee. Some employers consider 32 hours per week full time, but that is rare. Part time jobs require less than 40 hours per week of work.

The goal of most people who are looking for a job is to find a job that pays at least a **living wage** and also provides **fringe benefits**. A living wage is sufficient for you to support your household at a minimum level without going into debt. Many people who are working at or below the living wage must hold more than one job to make ends meet.

Fringe benefits include programs like health insurance, life insurance, dental insurance, retirement, vacation, sick leave, education programs, and investment funds. Each employer offers a different combination of benefits. Larger employers are typically able to offer more comprehensive benefits than smaller employers because of the **economies of scale** the larger employers can take advantage of. While benefits are not cash in your pocket, they do provide essential services, such as access to health care, that are very expensive for the individual to purchase. Many employers

Money Matters 32

Did you know that fringe benefits, such as health insurance and retirement, can increase the total compensation you receive by 50%?

pay benefits costs that equal an additional 30-50% of the employee's wages. So, if you make $10,000 a year and your employer provides fringe benefits worth 40% of your wage, your total compensation (wage plus fringe benefits) is actually $14,000 a year. This is a significant consideration when looking for a job, especially if you have a family to support. Fringe benefits can also eliminate the need for you to have a second job to pay for health insurance, for example.

There are a many people who are self-employed. This means they own their own businesses, which generate the income they use to support their households. This can be a very challenging, if rewarding, way to earn a living. A self-employed person must be willing to take risk and also be a jack-of-all-trades. The risk in being self-employed is that you do not have the cushion of the fringe benefits of a larger employer until the business is well established. Even then, the fringe benefits may be too costly for the business to support.

People earn money in other ways than working. For example, if you have grandparents who are retired, they probably do not work. If they do work, it is likely they only work a few hours a week. They have worked for many years. During that time, their employer was putting money into a pension, or retirement fund. Hopefully your grandparents also invested money in various savings programs to supplement their pension. In addition to the pension plan and personal savings, your grandparents may also be eligible to collect some **Social Security** payments from the federal government. Other people who are eligible for Social Security are people with disabilities that prevent them from holding a job and children whose parents are not able to care for them.

The independently wealthy do not have to hold jobs to earn income, although many do choose to work for the intellectual and professional challenge the work provides.

Their wealth is invested in various financial instruments to earn them enough interest income to support their lifestyles. Many times people who are independently wealthy will engage in **philanthropic** activities to help the community they live in or a charity they support. Bill and Melinda Gates founded the highly visible Gates Foundation, using the money Bill earned as a founder of Microsoft.

The internet has changed how people earn money. Have you heard of eBay? A lot of people are selling and buying things on eBay in hopes of making a good income or getting a good deal. This is like an electronic yard sale in that you never know what you will find to sell on eBay or to buy from it. It is important to know that a few people have been very successful making money this way, but most people do not earn much income this way.

This brings me to another way people try to make money. There are a number of businesses that recruit people to sell their products at home shows and recruit more people into the business to do the same. The person making the sale gets a percent of the sale as income, the people above him in the organization get a cut, and so on up the line. Do you see how it is obvious that the person at the top of the organization will make the most money, even being paid a very small percentage of each sale, because of the sheer number of people making sales, while the new salesman gets a percent of his sales only as income? These can be great opportunities for the right person, but not everyone.

There are probably still people in the world whose source of income is a mystery to you. This is often a mystery to everyone else, too, except the person himself.

How do these ways of earning money differ?

Some of the differences in how people earn money are obvious. Some people have to work and others live on interest income. Others are retired and are paid an income

---

Money Matters 33

Did you know that the average working American will hold 10-12 jobs and have 3-5 careers during his or her lifetime?

from their employer's pension plan, investment income, and Social Security. Those who are unable to work are eligible for some support from the government in the form of Social Security and other forms of social insurance.

Other differences may not be so obvious. People who do not have fringe benefits at work may have to "earn" their fringe benefits by working a second job so they can pay for them independently. If they do not have a pension plan or savings for retirement, they will have to continue working long after other people their age have stopped to ensure they have income. Even if they do have a pension plan, if they do not have good health insurance as part of the plan, they may need to work to pay for health insurance.

Summary:

In summary, we have discussed a number of different ways people earn money. Some folks have to work for it, others have retirement pensions, and others still are able to live off of interest income from the wealth they have invested. For those of you who need to work, it is important to consider both the wage and the fringe benefits when looking at the total compensation you are being offered. Sometimes the benefits are worth more than the wage itself, making the job worth considering.

Concept Reinforcement

1. How do people earn money?

2. List how these ways of earning money differ.

SECTION 2.3 - INTRODUCTION TO TAXES

Section Objectives:

- List the primary taxes in the US.

- Discuss how the various taxes are used to benefit society.

Introduction:

Taxes are part of life for everyone in this country. Americans pay a significant portion of their income to taxes, but not as much as some other countries, such as Sweden or the United Kingdom. There are many types of taxes: income tax, property tax, Social Security tax, Medicare tax, sales tax, duty tax on imports (tariff), capital gains tax, and estate tax, to name a few. The money collected through each tax mechanism serves a societal purpose, for example, funding medical care for those who are retired or in need of assistance. In this section, we will define the primary taxes you are likely to have to pay and discuss their purposes.

Types of taxes:

Income Tax: Income tax is levied on the federal level for all citizens of the US. Most states impose an income tax, but not all states. Some cities even impose some sort of city tax on income. The most common, however, are state and federal income taxes. Income tax is calculated based on **income.** There are several different **tax brackets** that are used to determine the percent of tax paid by the household. Lower incomes incur a lower tax rate (10% is the bottom rate). Higher tax brackets (higher incomes) incur a higher tax rate, to a maximum of 35% of income.

2008 federal income tax brackets

Income range – Single Taxpayers	Income range – Married couples, filing jointly	Income range – married couples filing separately	Income range – heads of household	Tax bracket
$0 - $8,025	$0 - $16,050	$0 - $8,025	$0 - $11,450	10%
$8,026 - $32,550	$16,051 - $65,100	$8,026 - $32,550	$11,451 - $43,650	15%
$32,551 - $78,850	$65,101 - $131,450	$32,551 - $65,725	$43,651 - $112,650	25%
$78,851 - $164,550	$131,451 - $200,300	$65,726 - $100,150	$112,651 - $182,400	28%
$164,551 - $357,700	$200,301 - $357,700	$100,151 - $178,850	$182,401 - $357,700	33%
$357,701 – up	$357,701 – up	$178,851 – up	$357,701 – up	35%

Federal income taxes are used to fund federal government operations, as state income taxes are used to fund state government operations. Income taxes fund government agencies, social welfare programs, research programs, military activities, etc.

Federal Insurance Contributions Act (FICA): FICA funds a **social insurance** program that includes Federal Old-Age, Survivors and Disability Insurance; Unemployment Insurance; Temporary Assistance to Needy Families; Health Insurance for the Aged and Disabled (Medicare); Grants to States for Medical Assistance Programs (Medicaid); the State Children's Health Insurance Program (SCHIPP): and Supplemental Security Income (SSI). As you may have figured out from the list of programs funded by FICA, social insurance is a mechanism that provides funds to the government to care for those who are retired (minimum age of eligibility is 62 for reduced benefits; 65 is the age for full benefits), eligible for a survivor benefit, are unable to work due to illness or disability, and children. Social

security tax is limited to a total of 12.4% up to $97,500 (2007). Medicare is limited to 2.9% of income. The burden is shared equally between employee and employer, which means that half of the tax is levied on the employee and half on the employer.

Sales Tax is a consumption tax paid on purchases for certain goods and services. The sales tax rate is set by the government. In Wisconsin, for example, the state sales tax rate is 5% of taxable sales. If you happen to live in Madison, the city has levied an additional .5% sales tax, which means that any purchases of taxable items in Madison will incur a 5.5% sales tax. There are some exceptions to the sales tax rule, for example non-profit organizations are usually exempt from paying sales tax, but this must be determined based on the tax law of the area you are doing business in. Many people consider sales tax a **regressive** tax, meaning that lower income people tend to spend a greater percentage of their income on taxable sales. There is debate on this issue, including discussion on whether the tax is regressive based on gross income or

> **Money Matters 35**
>
> *Did you know that the first permanent income tax in the US was established in 1913 when the 16th amendment to the Constitution was ratified?*

progressive on consumption based on rebates or exemptions. In many places, **necessary goods**, such as groceries, are not subject to sales tax. Sales tax is used to fund government operations. It is not allocated to a specific program as FICA taxes are.

Property tax is levied based on the taxable value of the property. There are three types of property: land, improvements to land, and personal. Land is the area of the property. For example, this author owns a home and also some investment property. Both the home and investment property include land. The home also includes improvements to land (the house I live in). The third category of personal prop-

erty refers to movable, manmade items. The taxable value of the property is determined by an assessor, who is usually a government employee whose job is to figure out the value of property with in the jurisdiction he or she works for. The property tax rate is described as a mill rate, which reflects the amount of tax per thousand dollars of property value. Property tax is used to fund school operations and other costs related to running the local government.

We have talked about a few of the many taxes you will encounter in your life. The taxes we have discussed are the ones you are most likely to pay as you establish yourself as a contributing member of the economy. Keep in mind that taxes pay for the services we take for granted from the government, such as schools, the military, and emergency workers. The government would not be able to provide these services if the workers did not pay taxes. It is important to maintain this perspective when you get into discussions of taxes with your friends and family.

Concept Reinforcement

1. Do you see the relationships between tax rates and filing status in the above table? Describe what you see.

2. If a property is worth $25,000 and the mill rate is 15%, calculate the property tax.

Did you know that ancient Greeks revered the tax professional as the most noble man in society?

SECTION 2.4 – WAYS TO EARN MONEY

Section Objectives:

- Define the essential difference between money earned on a job and through investments.
- Define tax-deferred investment and why this is an important savings tool.

Introduction:

As you have learned, you have the opportunity to make the most of your financial future if you plan well and have discipline. This lesson will talk about two ways to earn money: working at a job and making an investment.

I am sure that all of you know people who work at jobs where they earn an **hourly wage** or a **salary**. Do you know of any people who do not have to work because they earn enough income from their **investments** to allow them the freedom of not having a job? Most people who are able to live like this have either worked long enough that they are able to retire or they are independently wealthy, either through inheritance or as the result of a very successful business.

What is a job? A job is an arrangement where you are paid to provide a specific service to your employer. For example, some of you may have part time jobs delivering papers or babysitting. The service you provide benefits the business or person who pays you for it. The newspaper benefits from you delivering the papers to its customers and you benefit by receiving payment for the service provided. The same applies to babysitting. In exchange for you taking care of someone's child, or children, you are paid a certain amount of money. You might be paid by the hour or by the job.

Many people have **careers**, which consist of a series of different jobs in a general field of expertise. An example is accounting. An accountant may have several different jobs or employers, but has a career in accounting as long as that is the type of work she is doing. Other people may simply have a series of different jobs. Yet other people may switch careers once, twice, or more in their working lives. These changes come about because of dissatisfaction, new opportunities, or a desire for change.

A small percentage of the population is born into money. Their families are wealthy and able to provide everything the children need to live without having to work. This is the exception to the rule. Wealthy families will often set up trust funds to support their children throughout life.

Investing is a way to generate a stream of income that is separate from your job. Examples of investments include real estate, stocks, bonds, mutual funds, gems, precious metals, etc. Most people invest their money in stocks, bonds, mutual funds and real estate. These investments usually gain value over time. These gains in value occur in a number of ways. Real estate typically gains value over time. There are some markets that have rapid growth in property value and others that do not. It is important to know if the property is in a market that is **overvalued**. If the property is overvalued, you are less likely to make a profit on it when you sell. Undervalued property, such as property in an area that will be redeveloped, provides an excellent opportunity to gain value in the real estate market.

Stocks are issued by a publicly owned company to fund its operations. A share of stock represents one unit of ownership of the company. The majority owner of a company owns at least 51% of the stock, which gives the majority owner control of the company. Stocks typically generate dividends, which are based on the performance of the company over the past time period (quarter, year, etc.). Stocks tend to be more volatile than bonds because they are based on the economy. **Bonds** are issued by various governmental agencies to fund school building, the military, and other needs. Bonds are guaranteed a certain return, which tends to be lower than the return on the stock market, because bonds carry little to no risk. Bonds are purchased at some value lower than the face value. After the specified term (5, 10, 20, 25, 50 years, etc), the bond can be redeemed for its face value. For example a $20 bond purchased in 2000 that has a 10-year term can be redeemed for $20 after 10 years. The cost of the bond would have been much less than $20. A bond is a loan to the government or other issuing entity that has a guaranteed return on investment over time.

Money Matters 38

Did you know the first paper currency issued by the Department of the Treasury was the Demand Note Series 1861??

Money Matters 39

Did you know that currency notes are made of 25% linen and 75% cotton?

Investments can be made with **pre-tax** and **post-tax** dollars. Investments made with pre-tax dollars maximize the amount of money you are able to invest over time because the money invested is not taxed before you invest it, and withdrawals are subject to income tax when withdrawn by the investor. The taxation applies to both the principal and the interest earned. Investments made with post-tax dollars are subject to different tax requirements. Taxes are paid only on the interest earned, not on the principal invested. Why is this? Because the principal has already been taxed. Think about the difference in the amount of money you could invest pre-tax versus the amount you can invest post-tax with the same income. If you invest pretax, you are able to take money from your gross income, put it into the investment, and pay taxes only when you withdraw the funds. The limitations of pre-tax investment are that you are able to invest in specific qualified investments only and are unable to withdraw funds before age 59 ½ without paying a substantial penalty. If you invest post-tax, you pay taxes only on the gains (interest earned) on your investment. What is the difference? If you are in the 25% tax bracket and want to invest money, you can invest $100 pre-tax (from your gross income) or $75 post-tax (from your net income). You can already see the difference in the amount being invested. If you think about compound interest, imagine the difference this would make to you over the long term. What about taxes? Deferring payment of taxes until retirement may actually reduce the amount you pay because you will likely be in a lower tax bracket in retirement than you are when you are working.

Concept Reinforcement

1. Define the essential difference between money earned on a job and through investments.

2. Define tax-deferred investment and why this is an important savings tool.

SECTION 2.5 –TYPES OF ASSETS

Section Objectives:

- Define liquid asset.

- Define non-liquid asset.

- Discuss the differences between liquid and non-liquid assets.

- Define diversification.

Introduction:

An **asset** is something of value that you own. Examples include real estate, vehicles, bank accounts, mutual funds, retirement funds, life insurance, stocks, bonds, jewelry, precious metals, art, antiques, intellectual property, and businesses, among many others. For example, your parents probably have assets that include a home, a car or truck, bank accounts, and retirement funds. They may also have other assets – each family is different.

There are two types of assets: **liquid assets** and **non-liquid assets**. Liquid assets are assets you are able to access immediately if you need to use them for something. A widely used example is a checking account. A checking account is set up specifically to allow you to gain access to your money by using either a check or a debit card. **Checks** are financial instruments that allow you to designate the payee (person or business paid by you) and the dollar amount of the transaction on the check, which can then be cashed by the payee. Checks are printed for individual checking ac- counts, so you can use them to draw funds from only that account. It is important to make sure you have sufficient funds in your checking account when writing a check. If you write a check for more money than you have available in the checking account, you will be assessed an insufficient funds, or bounced check, fee by the bank. This also has a negative effect on your credit rating. Other examples of liquid assets are savings accounts, money market accounts, and non-monetary assets that can be sold quickly.

> **Money Matters 40**
>
> *Did you know that the term "blue chip stock" is based on the fact that blue poker chips are the most valuable?*

Assets that are not liquid include those that take time to sell, are difficult to sell, or which will lose value if you sell them prematurely. Examples of non-liquid assets include homes, retirement funds, businesses, and property, among others. Think about why these particular assets might be considered non-liquid. Let's start with homes. A home is the largest purchase a person usually makes in his lifetime. Purchase of a home typically requires the purchaser to take out a loan with a term of 15 years or more. This is something that requires significant planning. Selling a home usually takes time because the person currently in the home must find another place to live, the home must be cleaned out and made ready for showing, and then, once someone makes an offer (days, months or sometimes years later), the purchaser has to have financing, inspections, and other things in place before the sale can be closed (finalized) and the new owner moves in. A house may either gain or lose value during the sale process, depending upon whether the housing market is strong (increasing in value) or slow (housing maintains or loses value).

Retirement funds are assets that are invested for the long term and have certain restrictions on how and when they can be used. Retirement funds (IRAs and 401k investments) are not available to the investor until age 59 ½ without incurring a penalty. The government imposes significant penalties to those who choose to withdraw money from retirement funds before they reach retirement age. People whose short-term financial need is more pressing than maintaining the long-term investment have to pay substantial tax penalties for withdrawing retirement funds early.

Social Security benefits are available at age 62 or 65. The age at which you elect to collect Social Security benefits will determine the level of benefit. If you elect to start collecting Social Security at age 62, you will receive a smaller monthly benefit than if you elect to start collecting this benefit at age 65.

Diversification is the practice of insuring that your assets are in a broad range of investment types. Diversification strategies take into account the level of financial risk (low to high), the term of the investment (short to long term), and the goals of the investor. In personal finance, diversification means having sufficient cash reserves

66

(highly liquid asset), stocks, bonds, mutual funds, property, and other investments in an appropriate mix for your age and goals. For example, a young person is able to take more risk in investing than a person nearing retirement because the young person has many more years in which to recover financially if a risky investment fails. A person nearing retirement is usually more risk averse because this person will have to rely on investments to provide retirement income at a level that will support his/her lifestyle.

Risk, in terms of investing, ranges from low to high. Low risk investments, such as bonds, tend to have low financial returns (earned interest) and are very stable and reliable. High risk investments, such as certain types of stocks, are high risk, which means that there is a strong chance that the investment will lose money. People invest in high risk investments because the potential return is also very high if the company invested in is successful. One example is a company that is introducing a new technology, perhaps a new type of cell phone, to the marketplace. Until the new cell phone is accepted by the people who buy cells phones, the company does not know if it will be successful, therefore the risk of buying a stock in that company is higher than buying a stock in a "blue chip" company, such as IBM, which has a very strong reputation and track record in the business world.

> ## Money Matters 42
>
> *Did you know that Lloyd's of London, an insurance company established to share the risk of shipping, was started at Edward Lloyd's Coffee House?*

Concept Reinforcement

1. Compare liquid and non-liquid assets.

2. Define diversification

Section **2.1**

Section **2.2**

Section **2.3**

Section **2.4**

_____

_____

_____

_____

_____

_____

_____

_____

_____

_____

_____

_____

_____

Section **2.5**

_____

_____

_____

_____

_____

_____

_____

_____

_____

_____

_____

_____

_____

Additional Notes

_____

_____

_____

_____

_____

_____

_____

_____

_____

_____

_____

_____

_____

SECTION 2.6 –BUDGET

Section Objectives:

- Say why developing and following a budget is important.
- List the basic components of a budget (specific components of a budget).

Introduction:

A budget is a list of planned expenditures and income. A budget is typically prepared based on a specific time frame, such as a month or a year. All sources of income (inflows) and expenses (outflows) are identified in the budget with the plan of making the inflows match the outflows (making ends meet). Another way of defining a budget is planning the allocation of inflows toward expenses, savings and repaying loans. It is important to take pending patterns from the past into account. This lesson will take you through the components of a personal budget and why it is important to live within your income (living within your means).

Month	January
Gross Income	$2,000
Taxes (15%)	($300)
Net Income	**$1,700**

A budget contains several items that represent income and expenses. Each person's budget will be different because each person's life and needs are different. **Gross income**, **taxes**, and **net income** are the first entries in your budget. Once net income, or the amount available to spend, is established, you need to allocate funds to cover necessary expenses first. These include shelter, food, transportation, insurance (including health insurance), and debt repayment. There may be other necessary expenses, such as day care, that you will need to include in your budget. The budget for each person or household will be different. Some of the necessary expenses will be fixed, or the same, each month. A key example of a fixed expense is housing, either in the form of rent or a mortgage payment. Other examples include car and other loan payments, and possibly some utility payments (heat, lights, telephone), if you are on a plan that costs the same each month.

Month	January
Gross Income	$2,000
Taxes (15%)	($300)
Net Income	**$1,700**
Necessary Expenses	
Housing	($400)
Food	($200)
Transport	($200)
Utilities	($100)
Insurance	($100)
Balance	**$700**
Other Expenses	
Savings	($200)
Entertainment	($100)
Pets	($100)
Clothing	($100)
Personal	($100)
Other	($100)
Balance	**$0**

Money Matters 44

Did you know that manufacturing counterfeit US currency is punishable by a fine of $15,000, a prison term of up to 15 years, or both?

The second category of expenses includes those that are not necessary for your survival. These include luxury purchases, such as purchase of a new piece of jewelry or a trip. There are, of course, many non-luxury purchases that fall into this category, including savings, entertainment, pet expenses, and personal and other expenses.

We all need clothing to survive and not be arrested for indecent exposure, but the amount of money spent on clothing can be managed by how much you purchase, where you shop, and how well you care for your existing clothes. For example, if you need a pair of jeans and you want to maximize the "bang for your buck" by getting good jeans at a good price, where would you go shopping? Would you go to the mall? Would you go to a discount retailer? Would you go to a farm supply store? What about a resale shop? The first consideration is what you like, of course. The second, and as important, consideration is the budget you have to spend on your jeans. If your budget is $75 for a pair of jeans, you can go to a high-end clothing

Money Matters 45

Did you know that the United States Secret Service was established in 1865 and has a single mission of suppressing counterfeit currency?

store and look for designer jeans on sale. If your budget for the new jeans is $20, you are more likely to go to a **discount retailer**, **farm supply store**, or even a **resale store**. You can find some great deals on good quality clothing at any of these places, especially a resale store. This principle applies to any type of purchase you need to make. Some places will charge more for it and some less. You need to consider your needs, your budget, the quality of the item, and the use you will put it to when making your purchasing decisions.

Now that you know the basic components of a budget and how to figure out a simple personal budget, why do you think it is important to follow this budget? What do you think will happen if you overspend a monthly budget? How about if you overspend your budget 3 or 4 months in a row? It is important to live within your budget each month. If you break your budget once, you can usually recover if you are disciplined about how you use your income. If you continually break your budget without getting it back in balance, you will end up in dire financial straits, possibly including bankruptcy.

Concept Reinforcement

1. Say why developing and following a budget is important.

2. List the basic components of a budget (specific components of a budget).

SECTION 2.7 –ZERO SUM BUDGETING

Section Objectives:

- Define a zero sum budget.
- Discuss why a zero sum budget is important.

Introduction:

In section 2.6, we talked about the basic components of a budget. We learned about gross income, taxes, net income, necessary expenses, and other flexible expenses that should be considered when developing a budget. The topic of this lesson is to go into more detail on what a **zero-sum budget** is and why it is an important tool that will help you to maximize how you use your income.

You may have noticed in the sample budget from lesson 2.6 that the balance after all expenditures was $0. This is an example of a zero sum budget. If the person who follows that budget spends exactly the amount identified for each budget category, the budget will zero out, or end up with a balance of $0. This is great in theory, but how does it work in practice? Budgets rarely work out exactly as planned because we end up spending more or less money than we anticipated. This could be for a number of reasons: emergency, unexpected home repair, rapid change in price for an item (think of gasoline) that was not anticipated, etc.

A good goal to aim for in managing your budget is to spend less than you allocate for specific items, especially those in the "not necessary for life" category. Using our example of purchasing jeans from lesson 2.6, if you have budgeted $75 for jeans, but can get them for $40 on sale, you will have left $35 in your budget that can be

Money Matters 46

Did you know that the estimated budget estimate for the US in 2007-08 was $410,000,000?

applied to savings, to offsetting other expenses that were higher than anticipated, or left in the budget for the following month to help absorb costs. This is just one example. Another way to save money is to consciously minimize use of natural gas and electric in your home, as well as trying to minimize your use of gasoline by reducing how much you drive, carpooling, purchasing a very fuel-efficient vehicle, etc.

The minimum goal of a zero sum budget is to be sure that what you spend is the same as what you earn. Expenditures include everything from rent, heat, lights, and food, to savings and other investments. A zero sum budget is particularly successful if you are able to be as efficient as possible in how you spend money, which allows you to save more money for future use. It is possible to take this concept too far. For example, if you spend money only on essential expenses and save the rest, you are robbing yourself of the opportunity to attend concerts, give to charity, and buy things that you want, such as new furniture, travel, jewelry, etc. On the other extreme, if you spend more than you earn each month, you will end up in severe debt.

What would happen to the budget from section 2.6 if it is busted by $200 for one month, two months, or three months? How would you bring the budget back into balance? What happens if you are unable to bring the budget back into balance?

Look at the following table to see what the cumulative effect of overspending can have on the budget. There are variances in the dollar amount spent each month. In February, there is an unexpected car repair expense of $250. In March, the pet cat has an infection and has to see the veterinarian so she can get better ($150). April's budget is challenged because your aunt decided to elope and you want to buy a wedding gift ($125) to help her celebrate her nuptials. The bottom row of the table gives the cumulative effect of these additional expenses if you are unable to reduce expenses in other categories to zero out your budget.

Month	January	February	March	April
Gross Income	$2,000	$2,000	$2,000	$2,000
Taxes (15%)	($300)	($300)	($300)	($300)
Net Income	**$1,700**	**$1,700**	**$1,700**	**$1,700**
Necessary Expenses				
Housing	($400)	($400)	($400)	($400)
Food	($200)	($200)	($200)	($200)
Transport	($200)	($200)	($200)	($200)
Utilities	($100)	($100)	($100)	($100)
Insurance	($100)	($100)	($100)	($100)
Balance	**$700**	**$700**	**$700**	**$700**
Other Expenses				
Savings	($200)	($200)	($200)	($200)
Entertainment	($100)	($100)	($100)	($100)
Pets	($100)	($100)	($250)	($100)
Clothing	($100)	($100)	($100)	($100)
Personal	($100)	($100)	($100)	($100)
Other	($100)	($250)	($100)	($225)
Monthly Balance	**$0**	**($250)**	**($250)**	**($125)**
Cumulative effect	**$0**	**($250)**	**($500)**	**($625)**

As you can see from the cumulative effect under February, March and April, the additional expenses incurred each month add up to a significant amount of money, more than 25% of the gross income and over 1/3 of the net income per month. This is one reason to have a financial buffer in the form of a savings account, money market account, or other liquid asset that you can tap into if you have unexpected expenses. If you are able to recover from these expenses, you are more likely to maintain your financial health in the long run.

Concept Reinforcement

1. Define a zero sum budget.

2. Discuss why a zero sum budget is important.

SECTION 2.8 – DEVELOPING A BUDGET

Section Objectives:

- Develop a budget.

- Discuss how to track expenses by category.

Introduction:

Think about your personal situation. What kind of income do you have? What are your necessary and unnecessary expenditures each month?

If you are still in school, it is unlikely that you have any necessary expenses. Perhaps you bought a car that resulted in a loan payment. This would be a necessary expense because you need to repay the loan. In this lesson, we will develop a budget based on specific parameters you will be given throughout the lesson.

The first step in developing a budget is figuring out how much money you have available to pay your expenses, put into savings, and use for entertainment and other flexible expenses. We will do this based on some fictional numbers. We will use a monthly income of $2,350, which would be taxed at 15%. Let's figure out the gross income, tax paid, and the net income available to pay for your monthly expenses.

Month	January
Gross Income	$2,350.00
Taxes (15%) (gross income x tax rate)	($352.50)
Net Income (gross income – taxes paid)	**$1,997.50**

Now that we know how much is available for monthly expenses ($1,977.50), we need to deduct the necessary expenses that you will incur each month. Expenses that repeat each month include rent, utilities, debt repayment, etc.

For this example, we will use the following numbers:

Rent: $450/month

Utilities: $275/month

Debt repayment: $200/month

Transportation: $200/month

Let's see what this does to the budget.

Month	January	Balance
Gross Income	$2,350.00	
Taxes (15%) (gross income x tax rate)	($352.50)	
Net Income (gross income – taxes paid)	**$1,997.50**	**$1,997.50**
Rent	($450.00)	$1,547.50
Utilities	($275.00)	$1,272.50
Transportation	($200.00)	$1,072.50
Debt Repayment	($200.00)	$872.50
Total Fixed Costs	**($1,125.00)**	**$872.50**
Balance available	**$872.50**	

As you can see from the budget sheet above, once you have paid all of the necessary expenses, you have $872.50 remaining in your budget for other expenses. Keep in mind that each person will define necessary expenses differently. Some may include savings as a necessary expense and others may not.

The next part of this lesson will show you how other expenses can affect your budget plan. We will use the following numbers for other expenses, which are defined for this budget as savings, food, clothing and entertainment. Savings will be 10% of your gross income ($235.00), food will be $325.00, clothing will be $100.00, and entertainment will be $12.50. This provides you with a zero-sum budget.

Money Matters 49

Did you know that the President's budget proposal is not binding and must be enacted into law by Congress before it can be implemented?

Month	January	Balance
Gross Income	$2,350.00	$2,350.00
Taxes (15%) (gross income x tax rate)	($352.50)	$1,997.50
Net Income (gross income – taxes paid)	**$1,997.50**	
Rent	($450.00)	$1,547.50
Utilities	($275.00)	$1,272.50
Transportation	($200.00)	$1,072.50
Debt Repayment	($200.00)	$872.50
Total Fixed Costs	**($1,125.00)**	**$872.50**
Balance available	**$872.50**	
Savings (10% of gross income)	($235.00)	$637.50
Food	($325.00)	$312.50
Clothing	($100.00)	$212.50
Entertainment	($212.50)	$0.00

Expense tracking:

Now that you have established your budget, the next step is to figure out how you will track your expenses. In order to track expenses, you will need to save your receipts, organize them by your budget's categories, and compare your expenses with your budget each month.

One method used to track expenses is called the envelope method. Set up envelopes for your various budget categories with labels on them. In the case of the budget example we have just developed, the envelopes will be labeled rent, utilities, transportation, debt repayment, savings, food, clothing, and entertainment. As you spend money throughout the month, put the receipt for each expense in the appropriate envelope. As you go through the month, keep a running total for each category on the envelope and compare it with what you budgeted. If you see part way through the month that you are going to spend more in one category than you budgeted, you will need to decide whether to move money from another category to cover the costs, or change your spending habits so you stay within your budget.

If you see that you habitually overspend in a specific budget category, you will need to reassess your budget by changing how you allocate money to each budget category to be sure that you can live within your means.

There are other tools you can use to track expenses. Many people use paper forms to track their expenses. These are available at office supply stores. There are also software tools that are designed to help with budget setup and tracking. You can set up a spreadsheet on your own or you can get budget software, some of which will even download information from your bank account to give you a snapshot of your budget.

Concept Reinforcement

1. Develop a budget based on $2000 in income per month using the concepts in this section.

2. Discuss how to track expenses by category.

SECTION 2.9 –HOW DO I BALANCE A BUDGET?

Section Objectives:

- Balance a budget.
- Define debit.
- Define credit.
- Describe how to balance your budget.

Introduction:

We created a budget and learned how to track expenses in the last lesson. Now we will learn how to balance the budget.

The first concepts we need to discuss are **debit** and **credit.** These terms are used in accounting to describe removing or adding money to an account. A credit to your account means that money has been added to your account for some reason. This could be from depositing a check, earned interest, or transfer of funds from another account. A debit means that money has been removed from your account. Examples include checks that you have written on your checking account, automatic payments, banking fees, ATM withdrawals, debit card transactions, etc. Debits are shown in three ways: enclosed in parentheses ($5.00); with a "-" sign in front of the number; or printed in red.

We will use the budget developed in the last lesson for this exercise. Remember that this is a zero sum budget, meaning that we have allocated all of our income to pay for various expenses, as well as putting 10% of our income into savings for future use. Zero sum budgets are simple to create. It can be challenging to stay within the budget categories that you have established, so discipline in your spending habits is required. It is also necessary to review your budget allocations regularly to be sure that the budget reflects your individual situation.

Let us say that we used the envelope tracking method for our expenses over the past month. The envelopes have the receipts and running totals for each budget category, as below. Note that a new term, **variance**, is introduced in the table. The variance is the difference between the budgeted amount and the amount actually spent.

Month	Budget	Transactions	Variance
Net Income	$1,997.50	$1,997.50	
Rent	$450.00	-$450.00	$0.00
Utilities	$275.00	-$220.00	$55.00
Transportation	$200.00	-$210.00	-$10.00
Debt Repayment	$200.00	-$200.00	$0.00
Savings	$235.00	-$235.00	$0.00
Food	$325.00	-$350.00	-$25.00
Clothing	$100.00	-$125.00	-$25.00
Entertainment	$212.50	-$175.00	$37.50
End Balance	$0.00	$32.50	$32.50

In this example, we spent less than we budgeted for the month by $32.50, which leaves us with a **positive balance**. Do you see how actual expenditures varied in each category? Some expenses were exactly what we budgeted and others were either more or less than the budgeted amount. The net result, when we add up all the variances between budget and expenditure, is that we spent $32.50 less than we had available to us. We can either add the $32.50 to the next month's budget, we can move it to our savings, or we can use it to make an unplanned purchase in that amount.

Now we will look at monthly budget that is overspent.

Month	Budget	Transactions	Variance
Net Income	**$1,997.50**	**$1,997.50**	
Rent	$450.00	-$450.00	$0.00
Utilities	$275.00	-$300.00	-$25.00
Transportation	$200.00	-$200.00	$0.00
Debt Repayment	$200.00	-$350.00	-$150.00
Savings	$235.00	-$235.00	$0.00
Food	$325.00	-$300.00	$25.00
Clothing	$100.00	-$150.00	-$50.00
Entertainment	$212.50	-$225.00	-$12.50
End Balance	$0.00	-$212.50	-$212.50

Money
Matters 52

Did you know that $2 bills were first issued in 1862 and had a portrait of Alexander Hamilton?

Money Matters 53

Did you know Alexander Hamilton was the first Secretary of the Treasury?

Can you see where each budget category was under or over spent? Why do you think this might happen? Utility costs tend to change over the year, especially in climates with four seasons. The budget may reflect the average cost for utilities over the year instead of the actual cost for each individual month, and the expenditures for this period may have been for the coldest month of the year, which typically has the highest heating costs. There are likely to be months where utility costs are less than the budgeted amount. Of greater concern in this particular budget is the big increase in debt repayment. Does this mean that the person has added debt that needs to be repaid? Was there a one-time debt repayment, perhaps from a department store credit card? It is important to figure out what is happening here and adjust the budget accordingly going forward. Another category with a big variance is clothing. Expenditures are $50 more than was budgeted. Again, was this a one-time variance or does the clothing budget need to be increased over the long term? The last question to ask is how the negative balance of $212.50 is going to be covered. Will we reduce costs by that amount in the following month? If so, where will these come from? Looking at the budget, the food, clothing and entertainment categories are the easiest to adjust. It is possible to reduce food costs by cooking and eating meals at home. The clothing and entertainment budgets can be dedicated completely to covering the overdraft, if necessary. Keep in mind, however, that you need to be realistic when reallocating the budget from one category to another. If you will not live within the reallocated budget for the month, you are better off figuring out another way to make up the overdraft. One way to do this is to get a second job.

Concept Reinforcement

1. Define debit and credit.

2. Describe how to balance your budget.

SECTION 2.10 – EMERGENCY FUND

Section Objectives:

- Define an emergency fund.
- Discuss the importance of having a financial cushion.
- List some situations in which an emergency fund could prevent financial distress.

Introduction:

We have been discussing budgeting over the past few lessons. Remember that we consistently put 10% of gross income in the bank as savings. There are two primary reasons to save money. The first is for retirement and the second is to develop an **emergency fund**. An emergency fund is a liquid asset, often a savings or money market account, that has enough money to support you and your household for 3-6 months in case of an emergency, such as loss of a job, illness, or a family emergency.

Many people live from paycheck to paycheck, which works as long as income is coming into the household. If the income stops for some reason, a household that lives in this way will not be able to pay bills, will end up in debt, and will lose whatever assets they may have built up. An emergency fund provides a financial cushion for those who lose their **cash flow** over the short term.

Think of the expenses that you have to pay each month (rent, utilities, transportation, and food). There are sometimes ways to reduce these costs if you are in financial trouble. You can get a roommate to help with rent and utilities. You can reduce your use of gas and electric by lowering your thermostat, turning lights off when you are not in the room, and replace existing light bulbs with compact fluorescent bulbs. You can walk, ride a bicycle, or take public transportation instead of using a car. You can raise your own food, look for sales when shopping, and cook and eat at home. You cannot, however, completely dispense with these costs. You need a place to live. You need heat, light, and water. You need food. You also need transportation to get to work or look for work.

An emergency fund should, at a minimum, cover the absolute basics for your survival for a few months. If you can save enough to maintain your lifestyle for several months, you will be able to stretch the emergency fund over a longer period if you reduce your expenses.

Let's go through an example based on our budget from the previous lessons. The dollars available each month are income from an employer. The net income used to pay bills, etc., is $1,997.50 per month. In our prior examples, we set up a zero-sum budget to allocate all of the funds earned to different budget categories.

Net Income	$1,997.50	
Rent	($450.00)	$1,547.50
Utilities	($275.00)	$1,272.50
Transportation	($200.00)	$1,072.50
Debt Repayment	($200.00)	$872.50
Total Fixed Costs	**($1,125.00)**	
Balance available	**$872.50**	
Savings (10% of gross income)	($235.00)	$637.50
Food	($325.00)	$312.50
Clothing	($100.00)	$212.50
Entertainment	($212.50)	$0.00

The absolute basics (necessities) in this budget include rent, utilities, debt repayment, transportation, and food. Of these necessities, you need to consider which are **fixed** costs and which are **variable** costs that you can influence in some way.

Rent and debt repayment are typically fixed costs. Rent remains the same for the term of the lease, usually a year. Debt repayment is typically set up with standard payments over the period of the loan. Utilities, transportation and food are variable expenses and can be reduced through careful use of the resources available.

Let's look at our budget for these costs:

Month	Budget
Rent	$450.00
Utilities	$275.00
Transportation	$200.00
Debt Repayment	$200.00
Food	$325.00
Total Expenses	$1,450.00

How much money will you need to save in order to have a 1, 2, 3, 4, 5, or 6 months of financial cushion? The example below shows two scenarios: "Essentials" reflects the basic costs described above and "Regular" reflects the normal standard of living when employed. Do you see why it is important to conserve resources?

Amount required for financial cushion		
Months	Essentials	Regular
1	$1,450.00	$1,997.50
2	$2,900.00	$3,995.00
3	$4,350.00	$5,992.50
4	$5,800.00	$7,990.00
5	$7,250.00	$9,987.50
6	$8,700.00	$11,985.00

Money Matters 56

Did you know that 460 million pounds of button mushrooms worth $390,000,000 were grown in Pennsylvania in the 2001-02 growing season?

Concept Reinforcement

1. Define an emergency fund and discuss the importance of having a financial cushion.

2. List some situations in which an emergency fund could prevent financial distress.

Section **2.6**

Section **2.7**

Section **2.38**

Section **2.9**

Section **2.10**

Additional Notes

Money Management

UNIT 3

SECTION 3.1 - DEBT

Section Objectives:

- List types of debt.
- Discuss positive vs. negative debt.

Introduction:

Debt is that which is owed. Debt typically involves borrowing money, which is used to purchase a good or service that a person does not have the cash to pay for at the time of purchase. The consumer agrees to pay the lender a set amount each month, which consists of principal and interest payments, for a set period of time, or term. Debt can be a very useful tool in financial management or it can be the cause of financial ruin. It just depends upon how it is used and managed. The financial institution uses the item being purchased (car, home, etc.) as collateral, which means that if the borrower misses a payment, the financial institution has the right to take ownership of the collateral in lieu of payment.

There are different types of debt that people use. Each type of debt can have a positive or negative influence on the borrower. A positive effect of debt is to purchase assets, such as a home or car, which are purchased for a reasonable price. A negative effect of debt is when people abuse credit cards, purchase more home than they can afford, or buy a car that is too expensive. This leads to a debt spiral as people struggle to keep up with payments they cannot afford. This debt spiral can eventually lead to the person losing all of his assets because he has to repay the loan obligations he made.

Mortgage Loan: A mortgage is a loan taken out to purchase a home, which is usually the biggest investment of a person's life. The term of a mortgage ranges from 15-30 years. There may even be some with a term of 40 years. Many people have mortgages to take advantage of the tax breaks allowed for interest paid on the loan and property taxes paid on the home. A good rule of thumb when purchasing a home is to save enough money to have a 20% down payment before making a purchasing decision in order to save money on mortgage insurance. A mortgage payment typically includes principal, interest, and property taxes. The interest rate the borrower is able to get will have a big effect on the monthly mortgage payment. Do you think a higher or lower interest rate is better for the borrower?

Car Loan: A second large purchase that consumers often make is a car or truck so that they have transportation. As you have probably seen, vehicles are available in a wide range of price and function. The consumer is also able to choose between purchasing a new or used vehicle. The borrower often has multiple options for obtaining financing for the vehicle. New cars are often advertised with special financing deals for qualified customers. In fact, those who have the best credit have often been able to obtain car loans with 0% interest, which means they are borrowing the money at no cost to themselves. The benefit of this to the consumer is obvious – no interest charges for borrowing money. What is the benefit to the finance company? If the finance company is owned by the car company, such as GMAC (General Motors), the parent company often uses low to no cost loans to ensure that their vehicles are purchased and also to guarantee an income stream based on outstanding loan payments due to the company.

Car Price	$5,995	$25,995
Monthly Payment for 60 months	$99.92	$433.25

Personal Loan: Personal loans are taken out when someone needs cash for a specific purpose, such as a trip or big event, such as a wedding. Personal loans can be made either with or without collateral. Signature loans are made to people with good credit. The maximum dollar amount of the loan will be based on the credit rating of the borrower and the rules the bank has established for giving personal loans.

Home Equity Loans are a tool many people use to make big purchases while leveraging the tax benefit of mortgage interest. Remember our discussion about gaining equity – as you pay down a mortgage, you gain ownership, or equity, in the property. This equity can be used as collateral to purchase a car or make some other large purchase while keeping the tax advantages associated with a mortgage. Home equity loans can be a very positive tool for those who use them well. It is important to make sure you are able to make any loan payments required, especially if the home equity loan has a **variable interest rate.** Variable interest rates change based on the base rate used by the bank to calculate interest rates. The base rate is typically calculated based on the London Inter-Bank Offered Rate (LIBOR), which is the most commonly used basis for determining interest rates. Variable interest rate loans may seem less expensive in the short term than **fixed rate** loans, but can change dramatically based upon changes in LIBOR, or whatever basis the bank uses to calculate interest rates.

Credit Card Debt: Credit cards are a financial tool that must be used with great care. We will talk about them more in a later section, but the lesson for this section is to be aware of the interest rates charged by credit card companies. The interest rate can range anywhere from 0% for a brief period of time (teaser rate) to more than 20% per year. If you have $1,000 of credit card debt and pay only the interest for a year, that is $200 out of your pocket without making any progress on actually paying off the debt. That is expensive money! Many people get themselves in trouble with credit card debt and end up going into bankruptcy or having to sell assets to pay off the debt.

Revolving Credit Accounts: Revolving credit is typically store credit. For example, if you open a credit card with a department store, this is typically a revolving account with a high interest. This is nearly the same as a credit card, but limited to use in a specific store or chain or stores. It is easy to acquire too many of these credit cards as the stores offer some percent off a single purchase if you apply for a credit card. In almost all situations, it is not worth it to open these accounts, although you will have to assess this for yourself based on the particular situation you are in. Some stores may offer great benefits to cardholders. Others may not. It just depends on your situation.

Positive and Negative Debt: Remember that we briefly touched on positive and negative debt earlier in this lesson. The basic difference is that "positive" debt results in acquisition of an asset that is worth more than you paid for it in the long run. "Negative" debt is simply debt that does not result in acquisition of any assets. Can you think of situations that could be both positive and negative? First, think of positive debt. This could be purchasing a house, a vehicle, or property that is likely to gain value over time. Second, think of negative debt. This is more likely to be credit card or revolving credit accounts provided by stores. Credit cards are often used to make up the difference between income and expenses, which leads to a downward spiral of debt. Instead of getting into credit card debt, it is better to adjust your expenses to be less than your expenditures. This may require some belt-tightening or taking on a second job to pay off the debt, but it will be worth it in the long run. It is better to avoid negative debt, if at all possible.

> ## Money Matters 59
>
> *Did you know that nearly half of American families spend more than they earn each year?*

Concept Reinforcement

1. List types of debt.

2. Discuss the difference between positive and negative debt.

SECTION 3.2 –CREDIT CARDS

Section Objectives:

- Discuss appropriate use of credit cards.
- List ways people use credit cards well.
- List ways people use credit cards poorly and end up in financial trouble.

Introduction:

The first objective of this section is to define what a credit card is. A credit card is a form of **revolving credit** that accrues interest on balances that have not been paid off within the **grace period**. The issuer of the credit card lends money to the credit card holder (the consumer). The issuer pays the merchant for the purchases of the consumer, which the consumer agrees to pay back to the issuer of the credit card, based on specific terms. If you pay your **balance**, or amount due, every month (within the grace period), no interest will be assessed on the balance. If you do not pay your balance each month, you will be charged interest based on the terms of the credit card agreement. Credit card interest rates can range from 0% (short term **teaser rate**) to well over 20% per year.

There are also **charge cards**, which require payment in full each month. Charge cards are typically not used by individuals, but are used by businesses for tracking businesses expenses for employees who travel frequently.

Credit cards are used in lieu of cash for making purchases at stores, on-line, or when traveling. As described above, the credit card issuers essentially make a loan to the consumer by paying the merchant for the purchase, which then obligates the consumer to repay the credit card issuer. The consumer pays no interest if the debt is repaid during the grace period. If the consumer does not pay the debt in full during the grace period, interest is accrued, which must then be paid. Interest is typically accrued at a high interest rate, which increases the balance due, which increases the basis on which interest is assessed, even if the credit card holder does not buy anything else. The table below gives an example of the effect of interest. Do you see how making the minimum credit card payment costs a lot of money and takes a long time to pay off?

Money Matters 60

Did you know that consumers tend to spend 23% more when using credit cards than when they make purchases with cash?

The true cost of paying the minimum
Principal: $1,000
Interest rate: 18%/year, or 1.5%/month
It will take you 153 months (12 years and 9 months) to be rid of your debt. In that time, you will pay $1,115.41 in interest.

Payment Schedule

Month	Minimum	Interest paid	Principal Paid	Remaining Balance
1	$25.00	$15.00	$10.00	$990.00
2	$24.75	$14.85	$9.90	$980.10
3	$24.50	$14.70	$9.80	$970.30
4	$24.26	$14.55	$9.70	$960.60
5	$24.01	$14.41	$9.61	$950.99
150	$10.00	$0.54	$9.46	$26.38
151	$10.00	$0.40	$9.60	$16.77
152	$10.00	$0.25	$9.75	$7.02
153	$7.13	$0.11	$7.02	$0.00

*18% interest is the same as 1.5% interest per month.

**(2.5% of principal plus interest)

The next example will show what happens if you make a fixed payment of $25 each month without adding any new purchases to the principal. Again, using bankrate.com, we calculated the term and cost of paying off the $1,000 purchase using a fixed payment schedule of $25.00/month.

The cost of making a fixed payment every month
Principal: $1,000
Interest rate: 18%/year or 1.5%/month
Fixed payment: $25/month
It will take you 62 months to be rid of your debt. In that time, you will pay $538.62 in interest.

Payment Schedule

Month	Payment	Interest	Principal Paid	Balance Due
1	$25.00	$15.00	$10.00	$990.00
2	$25.00	$14.85	$10.15	$979.85
3	$25.00	$14.70	$10.30	$969.55
4	$25.00	$14.54	$10.46	$959.09
5	$25.00	$14.39	$10.61	$948.48
58	$25.00	$1.64	$23.36	$85.64
59	$25.00	$1.28	$23.72	$61.92
60	$25.00	$0.93	$24.07	$37.85
61	$25.00	$0.57	$24.43	$13.42
62	$13.62	$0.20	$13.42	$0.00

Money Matters **61**

Did you know that creditcard holders are not liable for more than $50 charged on lost or stolen cards?

Do you see the difference between how long it takes to pay off the credit card and the total amount paid in interest between the two scenarios? Do you see the benefit of paying off a consistent amount each month instead of just the minimum balance?

Scenario	Principal	Interest Paid	Total Paid	Time Frame
Minimum payments	$1,000	$1,115.41	$2,115.41	153 months
Fixed payments	$1,000	$538.62	$1,538.62	62 months
Difference	$0	$576.79	$576.79	91 months

Money Matters 62

Did you know that Diner's Club issued the first charge card in the US in 1950?

Let's talk now about ways to use credit cards to your benefit. If you begin to receive credit card solicitations in the mail, it is important to make sure you read the details about interest rate, teaser rates, benefits of the credit card program, etc. For example, many credit card programs include benefits for travel. If you like to travel and pay off your credit cards monthly, a program like this may be useful to you. Even if you do not pay off your credit cards monthly, this program may be useful. It depends upon how much you pay in interest to get the travel points versus how much an airplane ticket would cost you.

Another way to use credit cards to your advantage, if you are VERY careful in doing this, is to take advantage of teaser rates to pay off high interest balances. The downside to this can be damage to your credit rating because of the number of accounts you may need to open to pay off your balance without paying any interest. One factor credit card companies look at in determining your credit rating is how many **lines of credit** you have open at any given time and how frequently you open new lines of credit. Another risk with this approach is that you will lose track of how long the teaser rates are in effect and pay much higher interest rates than you might otherwise. Each situation should be assessed based on your needs, ability to pay, terms of the credit agreement and dollar amount of the purchase.

Even though you might think it is common sense to use credit cards wisely, it is very easy to get into significant credit card debt of $5,000, $10,000, or even $50,000. Think about what it would cost you to pay off $50,000 of credit card date at the minimum payment. The following table shows the details.

Principal	Total Interest	Total Cost	Months
$5,000	$7,115.42	$12,115.42	313
$10,000	$14,615.49	$24,615.49	382
$15,000	$22,115.70	$37,115.70	423
$20,000	$29,615.30	49,615.30	451
$25,000	$37,115.16	$62,115.16	473
$30,000	$44,615.58	$74,615.58	492
$35,000	$52,115.26	$87,115.26	507
$40,000	$59,615.44	$99,615.44	520
$45,000	$67,115.15	$112,115.15	532
$50,000	$74,614.83	$125.614.83	542

Concept Reinforcement

1. Discuss appropriate use of credit cards.

2. List ways people use credit cards well.

3. List ways people use credit cards poorly and end up in financial trouble

SECTION 3.3 –CHECKING ACCOUNTS

Section Objectives:

- Define checking account.

- Define direct deposit.

- List the four primary tools used to withdraw funds from a checking account.

- List characteristics of debit cards.

- Discuss appropriate use of debit cards.

- Describe how to balance a checking account.

Introduction:

A checking account is a **transactional account,** meaning that the funds in the account are safely deposited in the bank, yet easily available to the account owner. These are also known as **demand accounts**, because the money is available based on demand generated through check writing, ATM use, etc. The primary tools used to access the funds in a checking account are **checks**, **debit cards**, **direct debits**, and **automated teller machine (ATM)** transactions. Checking account transactions should be recorded in your checking account ledger, which is included with all check orders. The ledger allows you to enter each transaction with the appropriate details (date, type of transaction [check, debit card, deposit, withdrawal, account fee, etc], dollar amount, and resulting balance).

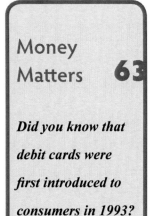

> **Money Matters** **63**
>
> *Did you know that debit cards were first introduced to consumers in 1993?*

Checking Account Deposits: As you might imagine, it is necessary to add funds to a checking account on a regular basis to ensure that there are enough funds available to cover the transactions that withdraw money from the account. Money can be added in four primary ways: **cash deposit**, **check deposit**, **direct deposit**, and **transfer**. A cash deposit occurs when you go to your financial institution with cash, complete a deposit slip that has your account number on it, and turn your cash over to the bank, which then adds the funds to your checking account. A check deposit works the same way as a cash deposit. In fact, you are able to combine cash and check deposits in one transaction. Another feature of this type of transaction is that you may request cash back, which reduces the amount of your deposit. This is particularly useful if you are only depositing checks and need some cash.

Direct deposit is exactly what it sounds like. This is an electronic transaction between your employer and your bank, in which your paycheck is electronically deposited in your checking account (or whatever account you designate) on your regular payday. Most employers strongly encourage or require this type of transaction because it reduces the administrative costs of managing payroll. The employer can generate an electronic transfer rather than writing  a check and tracking the deposit of the check by the employee. Can you see how this would benefit the employer? This also benefits the employee because the employee does not have to wait for the check to arrive or go to the bank to deposit the check.

Transfers are simply movement of funds from one account to another. Online banking systems allow account holders to transfer funds from one account to another, based on their need for funds. For example, if you spend more than you expect to in one month and your checking account balance is too low, you can transfer funds from your savings to checking account to avoid an overdraft. This can work the other way, as well. Setting up an automatic transfer from checking to savings can help you put money aside for future use.

Checking Account Withdrawals: A **check** is a paper financial instrument that the account owner uses to "pay" for a good or service provided by someone else. The **payee**, or person who receives the check, must then take it to a bank to either deposit the check in one of his accounts, or get cash in the amount of the check (cashing the check). Check use has declined since on-line banking has become available. Checks are relatively time consuming and expensive to use for paying a bill relative to a debit card or on-line banking transaction. Checks cost more to use because you must purchase the checks, and then, if you are mailing the check via the postal service, you must put it in an envelope and put a first class stamp on it. The payee must then visit a bank or mail in a deposit, which also costs both time and money.

Debit cards are plastic cards, which look like credit cards. When the user makes a transaction using a debit card, the funds are withdrawn directly from the checking account associated with the debit card. It is very important to track debit card transactions the same

way you track other withdrawals from your checking account to make sure that you stay out of an overdraft situation. It is also very important to protect your debit card from theft, because the transactions made with it withdraw funds directly from your checking account. If someone else gets your debit card and uses it, those funds are not available to you.

Direct debits are automatic payments (withdrawals) from your checking account. These are used for a number of purposes. Mortgage payments are often set up as automatic payments, as are contributions to charitable organizations that are set up for payment on a regular basis.

Automated Teller Machines (ATM) withdrawals: ATMs are a convenient way to access the cash from your checking account. There is typically a limit on the amount of money that can be withdrawn from your account by ATM transactions in a given day. The amount varies by bank and the type of account you have. An ATM transaction requires three things to be successful: a debit card, a PIN number (4 digit code), and sufficient funds in your checking account. It is very important to memorize and guard your PIN number so others cannot access your checking account if you lose

your debit card. It is also important to be aware of your surroundings when using an ATM to withdraw cash. They are a prime target for robbers.

Balancing your checking account

You will receive a statement from your bank each month for each type of account you hold. The checking account statement should be used to balance your checking account each month. Many banks are moving from paper to electronic statements. Regardless of the format, the bank provides instructions and tools to help you balance your checking account. The key points of information you need to balance your checking account are beginning balance, debits, credits, and pending debits (checks that have not been cashed, for example). Debits, as you learned in an earlier lesson, are the funds flowing out of your account. Debits result from store purchases, bill payments, account fees, and other transactions that withdraw funds from your checking account. Credits reflect the funds coming into your checking account (direct deposit, cash or check deposits, and transfers). The very basic calculation of a checking account balance is: beginning balance + credits – debits – pending debits = available balance. Keep in mind that your available balance may be less than your actual balance if you have written checks that have not been cashed by the recipients. It is important to include pending debits in your calculation so you do not get into an overdraft situation.

An example of a basic checking account balance calculation is:

$100 (beginning balance) + $200 (credits) – $150 (debits) - $25 (pending debits) = $300 ($100+$200) - $185 ($150 +$25) = $115 (available balance).

Remember that there are many types of debits and credits that can affect a checking account. It is important to make sure you include all of them in your calculations when you balance your checking account each month.

Concept Reinforcement

1.   Define checking account and direct deposit.

2.   List the four primary tools used to withdraw funds from a checking account.

3.   List characteristics of debit cards and their appropriate use.

4.   Describe how to balance a checking account.

SECTION 3.4 –CREDIT SCORE

Section Objectives:

- Define credit score.

- Name the three primary consumer credit bureaus in the US.

- Discuss how a consumer can use these agencies to maintain a
  healthy credit score.

Introduction:

What is a credit score and why is it important? As you begin managing your own money, it will be important for you to make sure that you maintain as high a **credit score**, or **credit rating**, as you are able to. A credit score is the result of statistical analysis of your financial habits, and thus your **creditworthiness**. Creditworthiness is an assessment of how likely a person is to pay bills on time. Credit scores fall in a range of 300 to 850, with 850 being the best possible credit rating. Most people fall in the range of 650 and 799.

Credit bureaus determine your credit score by collecting information on your financial habits, which they then feed into a statistical model that calculates a credit rating. Each credit bureau uses a different statistical model, so it is common for scores between bureaus to be different, often as much as 50 points, for the same person. Their databases contain slightly different information and their calculations may place more or less importance on specific measures.

There are three consumer credit reporting agencies, or credit bureaus that maintain information on individual consumers, in the United States. These credit bureaus are Equifax, Experian, and TransUnion.

Equifax (www.equifax.com) is the oldest of the three credit reporting agencies in the US. It was established in 1899, more than 100 years ago! The Equifax headquarters is in Atlanta, Georgia. This company gathers and maintains financial data on over 400 million people around the world. Imagine one company holding data on more people than currently live in our country! The power of this huge dataset is that it al-

> **Money Matters 66**
>
> *Did you know that in 2008 Minnesota had the highest National Score Index (measure of consumer credit health) in the US with a value of 721, as measured by Experian?*

lows the company to develop statistical models that are highly accurate in determining credit ratings for individuals.

Experian (www.experiangroup.com) is a global credit-reporting agency with operations in 36 countries. Experian maintains records on 215 million people in the US. This is not as many as Equifax, but still large enough to provide the statistical power required to develop useful credit scores. Experian was established in 1980 in Dublin, Ireland. An interesting service provided by Experian is a web site (nationalscoreindex.com) that shows average credit scores in a number of ways: region, zip code, and household debt. This can be a useful tool to determine how well you are maintaining your credit score based on your specific region or other measure. One thing to keep in mind when making these comparisons is that the web site does not cite the method used to calculate the score. There are several methods, as we mentioned above, so it is important to be sure you are comparing apples to apples when using this web site.

TransUnion (www.transunion.com) is the third of the " big three" credit reporting agencies in the US. TransUnion was established in 1968 and is based in Chicago, Illinois. Like Experian and Equifax, TransUnion is a global company. TransUnion maintains credit histories on approximately 500 million individuals around the world.

How can you monitor your credit score? The **Fair and Accurate Credit Transactions Act (FACT Act)** of 2003 is a federal law that allows consumers to request and obtain one free credit report per year (12 month period) from each of the three primary credit reporting agencies (Equifax, Experian, TransUnion). The credit reporting agencies partnered with the Federal Trade Commission, a federal agency that monitors trade activities, to establish a web site for this purpose. The web site, annualcreditreport.com, allows consumers to request free credit reports. You will need to provide some basic information (name, address, social security number), which allows the credit reporting agencies to provide your report. Keep in mind that the free credit report does not include your credit score – that information usually costs a small amount of money. However, the credit report will list your entire credit history by individual credit line. You are also able to request a credit report by calling 1-877-322-8228 or by mailing the Annual Credit Report Request Form to the agency.

Money Matters 67

Did you know that the Federal annual budget report in 2007 included an estimate that the share of national debt for every citizen in the US is now at $17,000?

Once you receive your credit report, it is important to review each of the lines of credit listed on the report. If you find a mistake, you are able to request a review of the credit line in question. You should make this request in writing to the credit-reporting agency, as well as to the lending institution. It is your responsibility, as well as the credit-reporting agency's, to correct any errors in your credit history. If you do not monitor this information carefully, it is possible you will be considered less "creditworthy" than you should, or, even worse, allow people to get away with **identity theft**, which we will cover in a later section.

It is important to use only the official web site when requesting a free credit report. There are imposter sites with similar names that will take you to web sites that are not the official FACT Act web site. Be sure to be careful when requesting your free report.

> **Money Matters 68**
>
> *Did you know that the printing presses used to print US Currency are capable of printing more than 8,000 sheets per hour?*

Concept Reinforcement

1. Define credit score.

2. Name the three primary consumer credit bureaus in the US.

3. Discuss how a consumer can use these agencies to maintain a healthy credit score.

SECTION 3.5 –WHAT AFFECTS YOUR CREDIT SCORE?

Section Objectives:

- List financial actions that have positive and negative impact on credit scores.
- Define FICO score and list the 5 primary types of information used to calculate the FICO score.

Introduction:

As you learned in the last section, there are three different credit bureaus that track credit activity and determine creditworthiness. Creditworthiness determines if lenders will actually lend you money, as well as the terms under which it will be lent to you.

Think about financial actions that might have a positive or negative impact on your credit score. The basic idea of obtaining and maintaining a good credit score is financial responsibility - for example, paying your bills on time.

It is unlikely that any of the students using this text have a credit score at this time. So, you may be wondering how to even begin establishing a credit history. One way to begin establishing a credit history is to open a checking account and manage it properly, being sure to avoid overdrafts. Of course, you must have a job or some other source of income to ensure that you can replenish the funds in your checking account as you use them. Proper management of a checking account will make it more likely that a bank will consider making you a loan or issuing you a credit card.

One trap to be extremely wary of when you are in high school and college is access to easy credit. Credit card companies often set up tables at universities in order to get students to sign up for credit cards in exchange for a t-shirt or some other gift. If you are able to manage how you use a credit card so that you are able to pay of the balance each month, it is a good way to establish your credit history. If you are unable to pay off your balance each month, your balance due will grow and you may end up in financial trouble because of credit card debt. Remember that credit cards typically charge a much higher interest rate than a bank loan, for example, and that the interest accrues on the entire balance (principal plus interest) for the previous billing period. If your interest rate is 18%, this will add up very quickly. Most high school and college students do not have much money. Because of this lack of money, it is very common for students to build up a substantial amount of debt just making small purchases or indulging in a little entertainment, like the occasional meal in a restaurant. Remember that if you charge it, you have to pay for it.

Financial behaviors that can help you establish and improve your credit score include paying bills on time, monitoring your credit report and correcting any errors you find, carefully managing the number of credit cards and other loans in your name as well as the number of "hard" credit checks by institutions to which you apply for credit, and generally living within your means (spending less than you earn). Credit checks made by lending institutions when they have received an application for credit have a direct impact on your credit score.

On the flip side, financial behaviors that will worsen your credit score include paying bills late, defaulting on bills or loans, applying for too many lines of credit or loans, and living beyond your means (spending more than you earn).

FICO is the most widely used method to determine credit score. FICO scores are calculated using five primary types of financial data.

> **Money Matters 69**
>
> *Did you know that only 13% of the US population has FICO scores of 800 and above?*

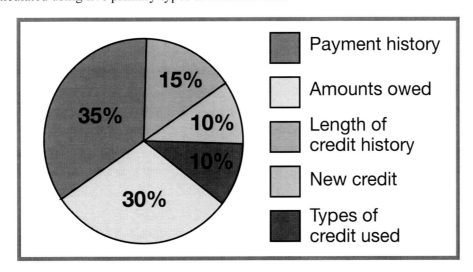

15%
35%
10%
10%
30%

- Payment history
- Amounts owed
- Length of credit history
- New credit
- Types of credit used

As you can see from the pie chart, each group of data is weighted differently, based on the importance placed upon that factor for the general population in determining credit score. Does it make sense that the two most heavily weighted components are payment history (35%) and amount owed (30%)?

Payment history includes information on the specific types of accounts you have open, any adverse public records, items in collections, and/or delinquent payments. Adverse public records include things like bankruptcy, law suites, wage garnishments, etc. Measures of delinquency include how long the amount is past due and the amount that is past due. Other considerations in scoring payment history are how long ago you were delinquent in payments, had any adverse public records or collections, and the number of accounts paid as agreed.

The amount owed assessment includes review of the amount owed on all accounts, how much is owed on specific types of accounts, the number of accounts with balances, the proportion of credit lines used, and the proportion of installment loan amounts still owed.

The other considerations, length of credit history, new credit, and types of credit used, are also important, but do not carry as much weight as the amount owed and the payment history. Length of credit history reflects how long credit accounts have been opened in general, by specific type of account, and the time since each account had any activity. New credit is just what it sounds like: newly opened accounts, hard credit inquiries, time since inquiries, time since opening, type of account, and re-establishment of good credit after getting past payment problems. The types of credit used is an assessment of the number of various types of accounts, including credit cards, store accounts, installment loans, mortgage loans, etc.

> ## Money Matters 70
>
> *Did you know that FICO stands for Fair Isaac Corporation?*

Concept Reinforcement

1. List financial actions that have positive and negative impact on credit scores.

2. Negative behaviors: paying bills late, defaulting on bills or loans, applying for too many lines of credit or loans, and living beyond your means (spending more than you earn).

3. Define FICO score and list the 5 primary types of information used to calculate the FICO score.

Section **3.1**

Section **3.2**

Section **3.3**

Section **3.4**

Section **3.5**

Additional Notes

SECTION 3.6 –IMPACT OF CREDIT SCORE

Section Objectives:

- Discuss how credit scores impact a person's ability to receive loans.
- Discuss how credit scores impact interest rates.

Introduction:

Now that you know what a credit score is and how to establish and maintain a good credit score, let's talk about the impact of your credit score on your ability to receive loans and how much those loans will cost you over time (interest).

We discussed the components of a credit score in past sections, and how some are weighed more heavily in calculating credit score than others. It is possible to be denied a loan, regardless of your credit score, especially if you request far more money than the lender feels you will be able to repay or you do not have a source of income. A poor credit score makes it difficult to get a loan for any amount, because the lender will be less certain that you will repay the loan on time and in full, and will charge a higher interest rate as a way to manage the high risk nature of the loan. In the example below, you see the financial cost of a poor credit score.

We will use a case study in this section. One person, Georgia, has an excellent credit score. The second person, Lucy, has a poor credit score. Both women want to purchase a vehicle.

Georgia's situation: Georgia has been very careful about managing her credit over time. She has established a strong history of making payments on time, living within her means, managing credit accounts and loans appropriately, has no credit card debt, and has planned her budget to accommodate the car payment. Georgia's credit score is 760.

Lucy's situation: Lucy has been living beyond her means and not established a strong credit history. She has a history of late payments on accounts, and has even defaulted on a couple. Lucy has not made any plans to incorporate a new car payment into her budget. She also wishes to purchase a new car. Lucy's credit score is 475.

Both women have the same income. They also both shop at the same car dealership and are looking at the same vehicle, which costs $18,000 brand new.

The only thing that is different between Lucy and Georgia, in making a car purchase, is their credit scores.

Variable	Georgia	Lucy
Credit Score	760	475

What do you think this means to the loan officer who reviews the loan applications from each of them? Remember our discussion of a credit score and how it is a statistical measure of the likelihood that the borrower will be able to repay the loan. Georgia has an outstanding credit score with a good history of payments being on time. Lucy has a poor credit score, which includes a history of defaults and late payments.

Georgia's application will be assessed as having a low risk of default because of her good credit history. Georgia is given a loan for $18,000 for a term of 5 years at 2.9% interest.

Lucy's application will be considered high risk because of her poor credit history. Lucy is given a loan for $18,000 for a term of 5 years at 10% interest.

The difference in interest rates is 7.1%. Lucy is paying more than 3 times the interest that Georgia is. The cost of the loan for Lucy is significantly higher because she has not taken care of her credit rating.

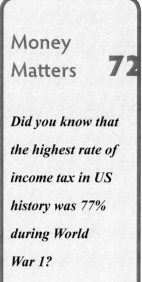

Money Matters 72

Did you know that the highest rate of income tax in US history was 77% during World War 1?

What do you think the difference in monthly payment and total payments will be?

Person	Monthly payment	Total Payments
Georgia	$323	$19,358
Lucy	$382	$22,947
Difference	$59	$3,589

Calculations made using the auto loan calculator at
http://money.aol.com/calculators/autos.

Money Matters 73

Did you know that the Civil War Income Tax was repealed in 1872, reinstated in 1895, and declared un-constitutional by the Supreme Court in 1896?

The difference in total payments made by Lucy ($22,947) and Georgia ($19,358) is $3,589 over the life of the loan. Additionally, Georgia's monthly car payment is $59 less than Lucy's. Looking at it from a different perspective, the premium that Lucy pays for borrowing money, given her poor credit history, is $59 per month.

The total cost of the auto loan is the amount of interest paid over the term of the loan, in this case 5 years. Georgia, with her low interest rate, paid $1,358 in interest over 5 years. Lucy, on the other hand, paid $4,947 for the same term and loan amount because of her high interest rate.

How do you think this might affect the long-term financial situation of each of these people? Georgia pays less interest, thus has a lower car payment, which means she has $59 per month more than Lucy to put into savings or some other investment. Think back to the discussion on long-term investment. Can you see how using the $59/month for investments rather than interest payments on a vehicle could impact the amount of money available for other uses, including retirement?

Concept Reinforcement

1. Discuss how credit scores impact a person's ability to receive loans.

2. Discuss how credit scores impact interest rates.

SECTION 3.7 –IDENTITY THEFT

Section Objectives:

- Define identity theft.
- Discuss how to avoid identity theft.

Introduction:

Identity theft is a term for crimes that occur when one person illegally uses another person's identity for some purpose. Identity theft is typically divided into four types: financial, criminal, identity cloning, and business/commercial identity theft.

1. Financial identity theft occurs when the thief uses someone else's identity to buy goods and/or services.

2. Criminal identity theft occurs when the thief poses as another person when arrested for a crime.

3. Identity cloning is occurs when the thief uses another person's information to allow the thief to assume the person's identity in daily life.

4. Business/Commercial identity theft is the use of someone else's business name to obtain credit.

We will focus on financial identity theft in this section. The most common form of identity theft is credit card fraud. The thieves purchase things using the stolen credit card information and the bill goes to the credit card holder, who is obligated to either pay for the charges or dispute the charges with the credit card company.

Credit card fraud is perpetrated in 2 primary ways: by stealing the card or by stealing the information about the card. Theft of the physical card often results in fraudulent purchases being made in stores, over the telephone or over the internet. If the thief only gets the information, but not the card, it will not be possible to make purchases

> **Money Matters 74**
>
> *Did you know the U.S. Secret Service is charged with investigating identity theft?*

in a store. Store clerks are often trained how to identify illegal credit card use. In fact, this author had her wallet stolen once and an alert clerk prevented the thief from charging some expensive items to the stolen credit card.

It is very important to report lost or stolen credit cards as soon as you are able to. This allows the credit card companies to inactivate the account so no additional purchases can be made on it. This protects both you and the credit card companies, who are diligent about monitoring the activity on credit cards for abnormal spending patterns. If an abnormal spending pattern is noticed, the company may contact the cardholder, or even lock the account, so no more purchases can be made until the cardholder is contacted.

Credit card fraud is bad enough, but identity theft can be much more destructive than a few illegal purchases. Thieves are able to use several different types of personal information to steal your identity. The information that is most useful for stealing someone's identity includes name, address, birth date, birth certificate, social security number, bank account numbers, and credit card numbers. Thieves have been known to go through garbage cans to get this type of information, which is why it is important to shred any documents containing personal information prior to disposing of them. There are stories of people who have spent years and thousands of dollars to reclaim their identities from those who stole them. This is very disruptive to the life of the victim of the crime, as well as damaging their ability to obtain credit.

How can you protect yourself from identity theft? First and foremost, it is important that you monitor your credit report and protect your personal information.

There are some specific actions you can take to minimize your risk of identity theft.

Be sure you leave your social security number, including the SSN card, at home. DO NOT carry the card in your wallet and do not share the number. Most systems that have used SSN as a way to

Money Matters 75

Did you know it costs an average of $808 and 175 hours to clear your name once someone has stolen your identity?

identify individuals (work ID cards, etc.) have been changed to a different numbering system to protect the SSN of the individual. This is because the social security number can be used to establish identity independent of other information.

Shred your financial documents prior to disposal. This includes bank statements, utility bills, old checks, credit card offers and any other document with personal information.

Protect your wallet. Males should carry their wallets in their front pants pockets, which are much more difficult to pick. Females who carry purses should be sure their wallets are secured in the bag, with the bag closed (zipped, snapped, tied, etc). Women should also be sure they carry their bags close to their bodies. If your purse has a long strap, carry it with the strap across your body and the purse itself in front of you. This makes it difficult for a thief to snatch your purse off your shoulder or slice the bottom of the bag to get your wallet. If your wallet is stolen, be sure to report it to the police immediately and report your credit cards stolen to the credit card company.

It is becoming common practice to write: "please ask for identification" on the signature strips of credit and debit cards instead of signing the cards. This obligates the clerk to request identification from you before the purchase can be completed. This also makes it nearly impossible for someone else to use your card because no one else looks quite like you unless you have an identical twin.

> ## Money Matters 76
>
> *Did you now that the government projects that identity theft crime will grow at an annual rate of up to 40%?*

Concept Reinforcement

1. Define identity theft.

2. Discuss how to avoid identity theft.

SECTION 3.8 – DEBT AND COLLECTIONS AGENCIES

Section Objectives:

- Define collections agency.

- Discuss the process of debt going to collections agencies.

- Discuss how to work with a collection agency to resolve problems.

Introduction:

If you get into debt that you are unable to pay in a timely manner, the person or business to which you owe the money may hire a **collection agency** to collect the debt from you. A collection agency is a business that attempts to collect debts owed by individuals or businesses. The collections agency is typically paid a percent of the debt recovered as a **commission**.

A collection agency is typically only called in as a last resort. The business will have gone through several attempts to collect the debt from the person or business that owes it. If the debt is not settled by a certain amount of time after it was due, the collections agency is likely to be engaged. The business will write off the difference between the amount owed and the amount collected by the agency as **bad debt** (a loss), which means that they no longer have to continue trying to collect on the account or carry the debt in their accounting system. Once the debt is sent to a collection agency, it becomes a **collection account,** meaning that the account reflects the amount past due (owed) by the person who incurred the original debt. Collection accounts appear on your credit report. Do you think this will be a good or bad thing? It is a negative in calculating your credit score, so it is a bad thing.

There are two types of collection agencies: first party and third party. A first party collection agency is part of or related to the company that holds the original debt, for example a credit card account. First party collection agencies are typically involved early in the debt collection process and will try for about 6 months to collect the debt. If they are not successful, the debt may be sent to a third party collection agency.

Money Matters **77**

Did you know most debt consolidation and counseling agencies were established by credit card companies?

Third party collection agencies are different, unrelated businesses from the companies that hold the original debt; therefore, they were not party to the original contract. These agencies typically work on a **contingency fee** basis, which means they are paid a percentage of the debt they successfully collect. The fees range from 10% to 50% of the amount collected, although the more typical fee is between 15% and 35%. Collection agencies usually try to collect debt by calling the debtor (collection call) in an attempt to encourage the person who owes to meet their financial obligations.

How does the debt collection process work?

The United States has strict rules in place about how the debt collection process must occur. Collection agencies hire attorneys who specialize in collections, who typically have a lot of experience in lawsuits filed to collect unpaid debt.

Steps:

> **Money Matters 78**
>
> *Did you know a credit rating agency is called a Ratingagentur in German?*

1.   Lawsuit filed with the court: The lawsuit notifies the person who owes money that a lawsuit has been filed. A **process server** presents the documents to the debtor to ensure that the notification occurs. Process servers may be local sheriff's deputies if local laws allow this arrangement.

2.   Response to the lawsuit: The person who owes money (the debtor) typically has an opportunity to respond to the lawsuit. This response must be filed within the time frame defined in the lawsuit or by local law. If a debtor responds to the lawsuit, the court will engage in a civil process to determine appropriate steps for dealing with the debt. If the debtor fails to respond, the collection attorney is likely to request a **default** judgment from the court. Default judgments are almost always granted in situations where the debtor does not respond.

3.   Once a default judgment is obtained, it is possible to obtain payment from the debtor using a tool called **garnishment**. Garnishment means that the court will send an order of garnishment to the employer of the debtor.

This order requires the employer to deduct a specified percent from the debtor's paycheck to pay off the debt. Federal law limits this to 25% of the disposable income of the debtor or the amount of earnings that exceeds 30 times the minimum wage. There are other limits on the amount of wages that may be garnished, such as if the person already has a garnishment in place or is earning less than a specified amount of money per year.

4.   A creditor may also collect debt by executing against a debtor's assets (cars, investments, property, etc.). If this occurs, the asset is typically sold, with the creditor receiving the proceeds, less any fees from the sale. If there is money left over after the debt is satisfied (paid off), the balance goes to the debtor.

As you can see from the process above, it is a large effort to collect debt from a debtor. Hopefully, none of you will get to this point in your financial affairs. If you do, however, it is in your best interests to work with the collection agencies and creditors to pay off your debt on terms that all can accept. This will allow you to slowly rebuild your credit rating. If you choose to continue down the path of unpaid debt, you are likely to end up in bankruptcy, which is the subject of the next section.

Concept Reinforcement

1. Define a collection agency.

2. Discuss the process of debt going to collections agencies.

3. Discuss how to work with a collection agency to resolve problems.

SECTION 3.9 –BANKRUPTCY

Section Objectives:

- Define bankruptcy.

- Discuss how to avoid bankruptcy.

- Discuss the impact of bankruptcy on credit rating.

Introduction:

What is bankruptcy and why should you care? **Bankruptcy** is a legal status that declares the inability or impairment of the ability of a person or business to pay debts (pay their creditors). Bankruptcy is typically filed by the debtor and is termed **voluntary bankruptcy**. It is also possible for the creditor to file a bankruptcy petition against a debtor, which is called **involuntary bankruptcy**. This is an attempt to collect some or all of the debt owed to the creditor.

Why is bankruptcy an option for a debtor? The first purpose of bankruptcy is to give

a debtor a chance to make a fresh financial start. The debtor must have made every attempt to repay the debts, but simply lack the ability to do so. The second purpose of bankruptcy is to allow repayment of creditors in an orderly manner, to the extent the funds or other assets are available to pay off debt. This occurs when a debtor has

assets that are liquidated to pay off debt in an order prescribed by the court. Creditors may receive none, some, or all of the debt owed when bankruptcy is managed in this manner.

There are two forms of bankruptcy: liquidation and reorganization.

Liquidation occurs when the legally unprotected assets (boats, rental property, recreational property, jewelry, etc.) of the debtor are sold to pay off debt. Creditors who have filed proper claims in a timely manner are paid in order of priority deter-

> **Money Matters 80**
>
> *Did you know that more than 1,200,000 people file bankruptcy each year in the U.S.?*

mined by the courts. They may be paid in part or in full if they have high enough priority. Those creditors at the bottom of the priority list may or may not receive any payments. A liquidation case in which no assets are liquidated and no debts repaid is called a **no asset** case.

Reorganization occurs when a debtor restructures assets and debts in a way that allows repayment of the amount owed, in full or in part, from income earned by the debtor while protecting assets as much as possible. This can save protected assets, such as a home, vehicle and tools of the trade, from being liquidated to pay off debt. This does not, however, mean that all assets are protected. The debtor's unprotected assets may be auctioned off and proceeds used to satisfy some of the debt owed.

How do I avoid bankruptcy?

Bankruptcy is not always avoidable, especially in cases where families have a sudden influx of debt, such as medical bills that are not covered by health insurance. If you think are getting into a situation that may lead to bankruptcy, it is important to be proactive in dealing with the debt. This is done by talking to the creditor about alternative payment plans, ways to reduce interest rate and penalty costs, such as late fees, as well as working with social service agencies to learn about government programs that may offer financial relief.

In general, it is possible to avoid bankruptcy by following a few simple concepts in financial management. We have discussed a number of these already in this text.

The most important way to avoid bankruptcy is to live within your means. If you spend less than you earn, you are unlikely to get into a situation where you have to declare bankruptcy, especially as you will have been saving the money you did not spend for a rainy day. If you spend as much as you earn, but are investing in assets, the assets can usually be sold off to avoid bankruptcy. You are most likely to get into financial trouble if you live beyond your income. Be sure to make and follow a budget that works for you, save money, make investments, and generally live within your means. If you suddenly find yourself in a bad financial situation, deal with it immediately, rather than letting it get worse over time. The sooner you deal with it, the sooner you will be able to move on.

Money Matters 81

Did you know that two Mae West movies, both released in 1933, saved Paramount from bankruptcy?

How does bankruptcy affect my credit score?

Declaring bankruptcy is a way to alleviate debt load for people who are unable to pay the debts they have incurred. As you might imagine, declaring bankruptcy will also have a negative impact on your credit score. If you declare bankruptcy, you will not be able to get a loan for seven years, during which time you are expected to make a good faith effort to pay off debt. Once the seven years have passed, you will be able to rebuild your credit rating, but will see that interest rates are higher than they were when your credit rating was good. As you repair your credit rating by paying off debt and establishing positive credit patterns, you should be able to obtain loans and credit cards at lower interest rates over time. Keep in mind that you will pay higher interest rates while you are recovering from bankruptcy, because you will be considered a high-risk debtor based on your financial history.

Money Matters 82

Did you know the average bank teller loses about $250/year?

Concept Reinforcement

1. Define bankruptcy.

2. Discuss how to avoid bankruptcy.

3. Discuss the impact of bankruptcy on credit rating.

SECTION 3.10 –HOW DO I GET OUT OF NEGATIVE DEBT?

Section Objectives:

- Discuss how to get out of negative debt.

Introduction:

You may wonder why there is only one objective for this section. The reason is that the objective is VERY important to your financial health. If you find yourself in a situation where you have accumulated a large amount of debt on credit card accounts or other non-asset building loans, it is critical that you reassess your situation and do all that you are able to do to pay off the accounts. This concept may apply even if your only debt is a mortgage, for example, because you may no longer be able to afford the payment required to meet your debt obligation.

How does one pay off debt? There are a few ways to pay off debt: second jobs, selling assets, and borrowing more money.

We will start with the last option on the list. Borrowing more money to pay off existing debt may allow you some time to figure out how to pay off your existing debt; however it is likely to cost you more money in the long run. This technique simply allows you to delay paying off debt until a later date. This is not necessarily a good approach to dealing with debt. A prime example of this is using low interest rate credit cards to pay off higher rate credit cards. If you simply move the amount you owe from account to account, you are likely to end up owing even more than you owed at the beginning because of transfer fees, accrued interest, and not paying off any principal when transfers were made. This is not an effective way to pay off debt unless you are very disciplined about paying off principal in the process. Even then, it is a challenging approach to financial management.

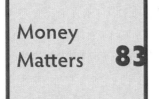

Money Matters 83

Did you know the London stock exchange was started in 1698?

Money Matters 84

Did you know the $100 bill is the largest denomination currently issued in the U.S.?

A second way to pay off debt is to sell off assets to get cash to pay off your loans. This is can be effective if you have assets to sell. If you do not have assets to sell, this is an ineffective strategy. Even if you do have assets to sell, this can be a very stressful way to cope with debt. It may include selling off vital assets that would be considered protected under bankruptcy guidelines, such as your home, vehicle, and tools of the trade. This is a decision that must be VERY carefully considered before selling the assets. You are likely to be better off following the next suggestion of getting a second job.

What is another way to help pay off debt? The simplest way to pay off debt is to reduce your expenses. If you reduce your expenses and add a second source of income that is dedicated to paying off debt, you will be relieved of the debt burden sooner than if you do not take on the second job. The key to success in this approach to dealing with debt is having sufficient discipline to use the income from the second (or third) job to pay off debt rather than for some other purpose.

What happens if you do not pay off debt and continue to accumulate more debt? You will enter into a negative spiral of debt. As you accumulate more debt, the amount of interest and penalties you pay will increase, and you will end up owing more debt than you started with. As the amount of debt increases, it becomes more difficult to make progress in paying off the debt.

Money Matters 85

Did you know the life span of a $1 Federal Reserve Note is 21 months?

Concept Reinforcement

1. Discuss how to get out of negative debt.

Section **3.6**

Section **3.7**

Section **3.8**

Section 3.9

_____
_____
_____
_____
_____
_____
_____
_____
_____
_____
_____
_____

Section 3.10

_____
_____
_____
_____
_____
_____
_____
_____
_____
_____
_____
_____

Additional Notes

_____
_____
_____
_____
_____
_____
_____
_____
_____
_____
_____
_____
_____

Money Management

UNIT 4

SECTION 4.1 –LONG TERM FINANCIAL PLANNING

Section Objectives:

- Define long term financial planning.
- Discuss the importance of long term financial planning.
- The rule of 72.

Introduction:

What is long term financial planning? You are all very young. Try to think 50 years into the future. You will be between 65 and 70 years old like your grandparents. How will you support yourself? Is there a particular set of goals you would like to achieve? Is there a minimum type of lifestyle you would like to maintain? What kind of retirement have you built through jobs (pensions, 403B accounts, etc)? These can seem like very distant questions when you are a teenager, but it does not take long for you to realize that you will be facing retirement before you expect to. This may also mean that you are facing the prospect of working longer than you would like to.

The standard age of retirement has been about 65 years old for a long time. Some people retire earlier and some later, depending upon their circumstances. There are costs and benefits to any retirement decision. If you retire early, you are able to collect less retirement benefit (pension) each month or may not be able to collect benefits (social security or payouts from individual retirement accounts) until a certain age.

Long term financial planning means that you engage in an active process of managing your income and assets to allow you to retire in the lifestyle in which you have become accustomed to living, or however you define a retirement lifestyle.

There are a number of financial tools you can use to plan your retirement. First of all, you are able to save money in a savings account. If you save a small amount each week or month beginning in your teens or early twenties, you will have accumulated a significant amount of money by the time you retire.

Money Matters 86

Did you know that American adults spend an average of 16 times as many hours selecting clothes (145.6 hours a year) as they do on planning their retirement?

Secondly, if you work, you will be contributing consistently to the Social Security program. This is a payroll tax paid to the federal government to ensure that those who are disabled or who have retired have some financial support. The amount of social security you are paid depends upon the income you earned while employed. Higher paid jobs will generate more social security benefits than lower paid jobs.

So, you know that it is important to engage in long-term financial planning. What does this mean?

It means that you are able to save and invest enough money while you are working to allow you to have a comfortable retirement where you will not have to worry too much about money.

What do I need to consider when planning for the long term?

The type of job you hold will help guide your long-term financial planning strategy. Are you employed by a business? Are you self-employed? Do you have income from a trust fund? The answers to these questions will help you figure out your long-term financial goals.

If you are employed by a business, you may have a retirement plan and/or access to a pre-tax investment account (401K, 403B) that allows you to set aside pre-tax money for retirement use. Remember that pre-tax money is income before income taxes are assessed and is used to build retirement funds.

If you have a retirement, or pension, plan through your employer, be sure you understand the terms of the program. Some programs allow you to **vest** immediately. Other programs may require a certain amount of time to pass before you are **partially vested** or **fully vested** in the retirement program. Partial vesting means that you have worked for an employer long enough to have gained partial retirement benefits based on your years of service. Full vesting means that you have worked for an employer long enough to gain full retirement benefits based on your years of service.

If you have a **trust fund** that provides some or all of your income, it is very important to be aware of how much you will benefit from the fund and for how long. Trust

> ## Money Matters 87
>
> *Did you know that the Lincoln Memorial is pictured on the back of a penny?*

funds are set up by the owner of the money or property to be put into trust. The terms of the trust are set up based upon the requirements of the owner and are administered by **trustees**, who are obligated to follow the terms of the trust when managing it. The **beneficiary** of the trust receives the benefit, such as income, of the fund.

All of these potential sources of retirement income, along with any other income/assets, need to be included in your planning. There are financial planning experts who are able to help you plan your financial future.

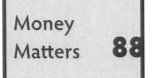

Money Matters 88

Did you know that the length of time a dollar bill is circulated averages 18 months?

Other things to consider when doing your long-term planning include:

1. What do you want to do when you retire?

    Different dreams have different costs.

2. At what age do you plan to retire?

3. At what age do you plan to apply for social security benefits?

4. If you have multiple retirement plans from different employers, how do they fit together to provide a solid income?

5. What do you want to plan to leave for others?

Now that you have thought about what you want to do in retirement and what resources you have available to save for those goals, how do you get there?

The Rule of 72:

We discussed the concept of compound interest in an earlier section, so you know the power of compound interest over time. **The rule of 72** is a method for estimating doubling time of an investment in years, based on compound interest. The formula is 72/interest rate = time to doubling. For example, if you invest $1,000 in a financial vehicle that pays 8% interest per year, how long will it take to double the investment? The doubling time (time for the original investment to double in value) is estimated using the following formula: 72/8 (interest rate) = 9 years to double. The doubling time changes based upon the interest rate. Look at the table below for a simple example of how interest rate affects doubling time.

Interest rate	Calculation	Doubling time
6%	72/6	12 years
7%	72/7	10.3 years
8%	72/8	9 years
9%	72/9	8 years
10%	72/10	7.2 years

There are other ways to estimate doubling time, some of which are more accurate, but also more difficult to calculate. The rule of 72 works well for estimating doubling times for interest rates between 6% and 10%. The formula is less effective as interest rates increase

Concept Reinforcement

1. Define long term financial planning.

2. Discuss the importance of long term financial planning.

3. What is the rule of 72?

SECTION 4.2 –HOW DO I PAY FOR EDUCATION?

Section Objectives:

- List 3 ways to pay for college.

- Discuss how each can affect long-term financial stability of the student.

Introduction:

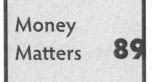
As you remember from our discussion on education and its impact on earning potential, pursuing education beyond a high school diploma increases your ability to earn money. Of course, the type of career you choose to pursue also affects this capacity. A physician is probably going to make more money than a nurse, for example, because of the differences in educational requirements and level of responsibility for patient care.

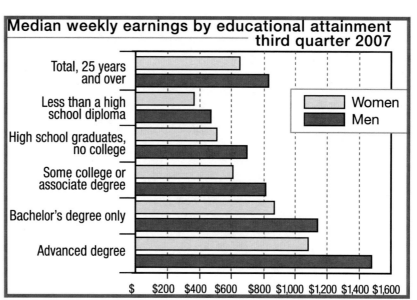

There are several ways to pay for higher education. Your individual situation will determine which strategy or combination of strategies will work best for you.

There are investment plans available for families to save money for educational purposes. These are called 529 plans, which are named after the specific section of the Internal Revenue Code that defines the plans. Money contributed to 529 plans grows tax-free and distributions, or payments, for educational purposes are not subject to income tax. Each state enacts its own laws to define 529 plans, which also leads to some variability in the details between state plans. There are two types of 529 plans:

pre-paid plans and savings plans. Pre-paid plans allow purchase of tuition credits at today's rates for use in the future. The value of the tuition credits in the future depends upon how much tuition increases over time. Pre-paid plans may be managed by either the educational institution or the state. Savings plans are investments made in mutual funds or similar investment vehicles. The value of the savings plan investments depends upon market performance. Savings plans are managed by the state. The donors, typically parents or other family members, may begin contributing to 529 plans as early as they wish in a child's life. Proceeds from a 529 plan will reduce the student's need for loans and other financial assistance.

Most educational institutions offer **scholarships** and other **grants** (gifts of money) to students based on a wide variety of conditions. Some are based on academic or artistic ability and achievement. Others are based on income level, membership in a minority group, agreement to join an organization (military, for example) upon completion of the degree, etc. Each scholarship and grant has different terms and conditions under which they are awarded. Scholarships usually require the students to perform at a certain level academically to retain the scholarship. Even athletic scholarships have these provisions. Grants are simply gifts of money given to a person for a specific purpose; in this case, helping to pay the costs of education. The long-term benefit of scholarships and grants is that they do not require financial repayment if you fulfill the terms of the award.

Student loans are available to students who need help with school expenses, such as tuition, books, fees, rent, food, etc. These loans must be repaid with interest once the student is no longer in school. Student loans often have very low interest rates and long repayment periods. This can lead to abuse of student loans because they are considered "cheap" money. It is important to think of the long-term cost to your financial health if you borrow more money than you need to get through school. For example, if you take out a student loan to do or to buy something that you do not need for educational purposes, it simply adds to the amount that you will have to repay, and reduces how much you will be able to save and invest until the loans are repaid.

Money Matters 90

Did you know a "c" note is a $100 bill?

135

Work-study programs pay students who qualify for the program for working at approved jobs. These jobs are usually in the educational institution. This is an attractive program for those in the university who hire the students. The work-study program pays the hourly wage of the student up to a specific level defined by the program. This allows a student to be hired with little or no cost to the employer. The student and the employer both benefit. The student has gainful employment. The employer has a double benefit: a good worker, and someone who costs little or nothing to the employer. Students who work at jobs have less need to borrow money to meet their expenses.

Non-work-study jobs also contribute to the funds available to meet expenses while in school. Any type of job (retail, restaurant, odd jobs, etc.) will contribute to the budget.

If you decide to go to graduate school to pursue a master's degree or a doctoral degree, you will have the opportunity to compete for a graduate assistantship. Graduate assistantships are typically for conducting research or for teaching classes. These assistantships typically provide a **stipend**, which is a payment made to the student by the school to help with living expenses, and often also includes the **tuition** payment for the student awarded the assistantship. If you live frugally, it is usually possible to live on these assistantships without taking out further loans.

Money Matters 91

Did you know that 2006 graduates of Embry Riddle Aeronautical University graduated with an average of $52,276 of loan debt?

Concept Reinforcement

1. List 3 ways to pay for college.

2. Discuss how each can affect long-term financial stability of the student.

SECTION 4.3 – PURCHASING A VEHICLE

Section Objectives:

- List considerations when purchasing a vehicle.
- Discuss the differences between lease and purchase.
- Discuss when leases are appropriate.
- Discuss when purchase is appropriate.
- List considerations in buying a new vehicle vs. a used vehicle.

Introduction:

You are likely to purchase or lease several vehicles during your lifetime. It is important to carefully think through the decision to acquire a vehicle, especially if you will be taking on debt to make the purchase.

Before you even decide whether you are going to buy or lease a vehicle, you need to think through your reasons for doing so. Do you need a different type of vehicle for your work? Does your existing car require expensive maintenance? If yes, will it cost you more than the car is worth to repair it? Do you just want a different vehicle? Have you had a change in your personal situation (marriage, children, pets) that changes what you need in a vehicle? Going through this thought process will help you define the type of vehicle you are going to acquire. You also need to consider how you will pay for the vehicle. We will discuss the options of purchase versus lease later in this section.

Once you have decided to acquire a new vehicle, have determined what kind of vehicle you need, and figured out how much you are able to spend, you need to do research into the vehicles that will meet your needs. It is important to look at reports of maintenance costs, reliability, gas mileage, consumer confidence, repair costs, warranty, etc. For example, if you decide you want a foreign luxury car, it is important to understand the maintenance costs for the vehicle, which are likely to be significantly higher than the maintenance costs for a similar American-made vehicle, and factor those costs into your purchase decision.

The next decision to be made is whether to purchase or lease the vehicle. If you purchase the vehicle, you own it outright once the purchase price is paid off. You can do

> **Money Matters 92**
>
> *Did you know that in 1901 Oldsmobile manufactured 425 Curved Dash Oldsmobiles, which sold for $650 each?*

this either by paying cash (if you've saved enough to do this) or through an auto loan. If you pay cash, you own the vehicle with no restrictions. If you take out a loan, the bank holds a **lien** on the vehicle until you have paid off the loan. This allows the bank to recover some of their costs if you default on the loan. Taking out a loan also means that you need to budget the loan repayment into your financial management plan. The advantage to purchasing a vehicle is that you end up owning the vehicle. You are then able to drive the vehicle as long as you wish and are able to keep it in working order. You may also then use the vehicle as a trade-in to offset the purchase price when you decide to purchase a different vehicle.

It is also possible to lease vehicles. This allows you to acquire a more expensive vehicle than you would be able to purchase, but also comes with restrictions. Leases are typically for a specific term, three years, for example. You will need to have saved enough money to pay for the down payment, title, and insurance. You are limited to a certain number of miles per year or lease period. If you go over that mileage limit, you will be assessed a fee for each mile driven beyond the maximum. This adds up quickly if you are charged $.15/mile above the maximum mileage. You will also need to include the lease costs in your financial management plan. The other option with a lease is to purchase your vehicle when your lease is up. This means that you either need to save or borrow the money to do so. Leases are good options for people who like to have a different vehicle every few years. The downside is that you always have to include the lease payment in your budget.

The other choice that you will need to make is whether you acquire a new or used vehicle. There are pros and cons to either choice. A new vehicle has many pros – a full warranty, no history of accidents or repairs, and you get to choose the options you want when you order it. Some of the cons of a new vehicle are the higher price and the "new car penalty," which is the drop in value that occurs as soon as you drive it off the car lot. Used vehicles also have pros and cons. The price of a used vehicle is usually less and you do not incur the new car penalty. However, you do not always know how the vehicle has been maintained, or if it has been in an accident. The warranty, if any, is limited, so you are exposed to the risk of paying for repairs immediately if something goes wrong.

Money Matters 93

Did you know that a 1953 Buick Roadmaster that once belonged to Howard Hughes sold for 1.62 million dollars at the Barrett-Jackson auto auction on April 2, 2005?

One of the best references to use when assessing the value of a used car is called the Kelley Blue Book. The blue book value is considered market value for a used vehicle. The value is calculated based on the make, model, options, year, and condition of the vehicle. The Kelley Blue Book web site is www.kbb.com and has calculators that will allow you to determine the value of the vehicle you are considering. There are three values calculated (trade in, private party, and suggested retail). For example, the blue book value of a 2003 Saturn Ion 3 with some options (as of March 11, 2008) is:

Condition	Trade-in Value	Private Party Value	Suggested Retail Value
Excellent	$6,000	$7,800	$9,680
Fair	$5,515	$7,220	n/a
Poor	$4,685	$6,460	n/a

Can you see the value in maintaining your vehicle if you are planning to use it as a trade-in or sell it to someone else?

Money Matters 94

Did you know that the Average Cost (Per Mile) of Owning and Operating an Automobile has increased from $0.14 per mile in 1975 to = $0.50 per mile (includes gas, oil, maintenance, tires etc) in 2001?

Concept Reinforcement

1. List considerations when purchasing a vehicle.

2. Discuss the differences between lease and purchase.

3. Discuss when leases are appropriate

4. Discuss when purchase is appropriate.

5. List considerations in buying a new vehicle vs. a used vehicle.

SECTION 4.4 –PURCHASING A HOME

Section Objectives:

- Discuss how saving for a home purchase can reduce overall home purchase costs.
- Name 3 key considerations in determining how much home one can afford.
- Discuss research the homebuyer should do to understand the real cost of owning a home.

Introduction:

One of the biggest investments many people make in their lives is a home. Purchasing a home allows a person to gain **equity** in the property as the mortgage of the home is paid down. This is different than paying **rent**, which is paying the landlord for the right to live in a property. Renting property does not allow the renter to gain any equity in the property.

The decision to rent or own a home is a big one. There are some people for whom renting a property is preferable to owning. These people include those who are unable to care for a home, or just do not want the responsibility of taxes, insurance, mortgage payments, maintenance, etc. Owning a home is a large responsibility and a lot of work. If you rent, someone else is likely responsible for maintaining the property, mowing the lawn, clearing the sidewalks, paying the taxes and insurance, and maybe even paying the utilities. If you own your home, unless it is a **condominium**, you will be responsible for all aspects of maintaining your home, paying taxes, paying utilities, and insurance. Condominium living is a balance between home ownership and renting. The condo owner gains equity as the mortgage on the condo is paid down, but also pays a condominium fee to cover the expenses of building maintenance, etc. The items covered by this fee are defined differently for each condominium complex.

Once you have decided to purchase a home, whether it is a condo or a home for which you do all the work, you will need to assess your financial situation. Saving a down payment of 20% of the sale price will reduce your overall cost in purchasing the home. Why is this? **Private mortgage insurance (PMI)** is required for homebuyers who mortgage more than 80% of the purchase price of the home. PMI protects the lender from default on the mortgage payment. PMI premiums are paid by the borrower to protect the lender. Do you see why the borrower would rather not pay this premium? The premium is typically ½ to 1% of the loan amount each year. If you have a $100,000 loan with PMI of ½%, the premium will be $500 for the year ($100,000 x .005 = $500 premium). If you did not have to pay $500 in PMI premiums, that $500 could be put toward principal or invested in a retirement fund.

How do you know how much home you can afford? The first thing to do is consider your budget. How much have you saved for a down payment? How much are you currently paying for rent? How much can you afford to pay for a mortgage? Are you able and willing to care for the property? Can you afford the home insurance? In many cases, the advantages of home ownership outweigh the costs.

How much mortgage can you afford? The example below was calculated using the mortgage calculator at the AOL Money & Finance web site. This particular calculator is used to figure out how much money you might be able to borrow, given your personal financial variables. http://calculators.aol.com/tools/aol/home01/tool.fcs

> **Money Matters 96**
>
> *Did you know that every piece of paper currency issued since 1861 is valid and legal tender?*

Here is the profile used to calculate the possible loan amounts.

Monthly wages before taxes or deductions	**$4,000.00**
Monthly Payments *	
Auto loans	$300.00
Student loans	$150.00
Monthly credit card payments	$150.00
Loan terms you desire	
Interest rate	6.50%
Term (years)	15
Down payment (% of price)	20
Taxes & insurance you expect	
Yearly property tax	$2,000.00
Yearly property insurance	$200.00

The amount you can borrow, based upon various down payments, including the down payment you indicated:

A Conservative Estimate				
Percent down	**5.00%**	**10.00%**	**20.00%**	**25.00%**
Down payment amount	$5,372	$11,690	$29,177	$38,903
Loan amount	$102,059	$105,211	$116,710	$116,710
Price of home	$107,431	$116,901	$145,887	$155,613
Your Future Monthly Payment				
Principal and interest	$889	$917	$1,017	$1,017
Taxes and insurance	$183	$183	$183	$183
Mortgage insurance	$48	$20	$0	$0
Total monthly payment	**$1,120**	**$1,120**	**$1,200**	**$1,200**
An Aggressive Estimate				
Percent down	5.00%	10.00%	20.00%	25.00%
Down payment amount	$5,830	$14,186	$36,065	$48,087
Loan amount	$110,775	$127,676	$144,261	$144,261
Price of home	$116,605	$141,862	$180,326	$192,348
Your Future Monthly Payment				
Principal and interest	$965	$1,112	$1,257	$1,257
Taxes and insurance	$183	$183	$183	$183
Mortgage insurance	$52	$24	$0	$0
Total monthly payment	**$1,200**	**$1,319**	**$1,440**	**$1,440**

Notice that the calculator gives both a conservative (cautious) and aggressive estimate of the maximum amount you might be able to borrow. The calculator also gives information based on different down payment percentages. Does this make sense given the concept of keeping housing costs below 25% of net income?

Let's look at the results from another calculator, this one from bankrate. com. http://www.bankrate.com/brm/calc/newhouse/calculator.asp

This calculator gives an affordable mortgage payment, which is different than the maximum amount you can borrow as the first one does. Using the same variables, the bankrate.com calculator calculated the following available mortgage limits:

Affordable monthly mortgage payment $656.67

Affordable home purchase amount $85,382.98

Look at the difference in the amount of the mortgage payment calculations from the two mortgage calculators. Now think back to the 25% of net income rule for housing costs and what the monthly net income will be based on a $4,000 a month income, which is subject to 25% income tax. This leaves a net income of $3,000/month. $3,000 x 25% = $750/month available for housing costs.

You may have noticed that the calculations above include some considerations other than mortgage amount and income. When looking at homes, it is important to understand the true cost of owning a home. Think about all the things that need to be done at home to maintain the building and the property. What about utility bills? What condition is the roof in? Will it need to be replaced soon? What about the inside of the house? Do you need to update the interior, kitchen appliances, furnace, air conditioner, etc? Is the driveway in good condition or will it need to be replaced soon? What are the property taxes? It is important to understand the monthly costs of running the home (utilities and maintenance) as well as any large repairs or updates that need to be completed before committing to a home purchase.

Concept Reinforcement

1. Discuss how saving for a home purchase can reduce overall home purchase costs.

2. Name 3 key considerations in determining how much home one can afford.

3. Discuss research the homebuyer should do to understand the real cost of owning a home.

SECTION 4.5 –RETIREMENT PLANNING

Section Objectives:

- Discuss the importance of retirement planning.
- List issues that need to be considered in retirement planning.

Introduction:

Retirement is a long way away for most of you, but it is important to begin planning for your retirement as soon as you are able to. Remember the Rule of 72 and the impact of investing for the long term. Each of you will probably work for 40-50 years. This will allow you ample opportunity to save money for retirement.

Why do you have to plan? Most people change jobs several times in their lives and are increasingly changing careers once or twice in their working lives. This is a very different scenario than past generations have faced. Many people would start working at a company right out of high school or college and continue working for the company until retirement. This allows the person to accumulate a substantial pension and retire comfortably even if he did not do much other retirement planning. The scenario people face now in retirement planning includes multiple pension packages from different jobs, various other retirement accounts, and an uncertain future for social security and Medicare benefits from the federal government. This is combined with a longer life span, in general, and increased costs of living and rapidly increasing health care costs.

There are financial planners who specialize in helping people develop retirement plans based on their personal goals. Everyone has different plans for when they want to retire and how they want to spend that time. Some want to just quit work and stay home. Others want to quit working so they can travel or follow some other passion. Yet others want to begin a second career that they may need to self-finance. Health status, health insurance, and long-term care needs are also important considerations. An increasing number of retirees have taken on the responsibility of raising their grandchildren, which requires that they have sufficient funds to provide the child or children with what they need as they are growing up.

Money Matters 98

Did you know that a stack of 14,500,000 bills would reach a mile high?

The first thing you will need to determine is the income you will need to support your obligations and dreams in retirement. This discussion will include all of the factors we just discussed, as well as any that are unique to your particular situation. It is very easy to put off retirement planning. If you do, you run the risk of being unable to retire when or how you wish. You may not even be able to retire at all if you have no resources to support yourself.

Think about retired people you know. Do any of them live on **fixed incomes?** Are they able to do everything that they need or want to do?

Your total financial picture for retirement, if you plan ahead, will probably include:

- Pension Plan Benefits, including years of service, vesting, and salary calculations

- Individual Retirement Account income (401K or 403B)

- Roth IRA income

- Real property, such as rental units, that will provide income

- Social Security Benefits

- Income from other investments (stocks, bonds, mutual funds, etc.)

The proportion of each in your retirement portfolio will vary for each person.

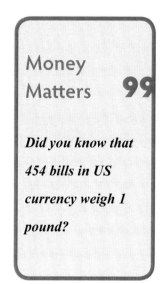

Money Matters **99**

Did you know that 454 bills in US currency weigh 1 pound?

Given that many people change jobs, and even careers, more than one time in their working lives, it is important to consider the retirement benefits accrued at each job (if any), retirement funds saved, anticipated social security benefits, and other assets, such as property, that will be used to finance retirement.

Pension benefits will vary from employer to employer. Some have no retirement plan and some offer **fully funded** pension plans. Most, however, calculate benefits based on a formula that includes years of service, highest salary or highest average salary over 2-3 years, and whether you are partially or fully vested in your retirement plan. It is important that you and your financial planner consider the benefits you have accrued at each employer.

Social security benefits must be included in your retirement income calculations, even though you should consider this supplemental income because of the current concerns about the viability of the social security system into the future. As you go through your working life, you will contribute to the Social Security program. The amount you contribute will be based on your income, up to a maximum amount ($102,000 in income for 2008) determined by the government. The Social Security Online web site - http://www.ssa.gov/ - provides calculators and information about the programs. This web site also includes information on how to plan for retirement, how to calculate Social Security benefits, Medicare, the future of Social Security, and many other topics.

We will look at various retirement investment vehicles and income sources in the coming sections.

Concept Reinforcement

1. Discuss the importance of retirement planning.

2. List issues that need to be considered in retirement planning.

Section **4.1**

Section **4.2**

Section **4.3**

Section **4.4**

Section **4.5**

Additional Notes

SECTION 4.6 –STOCKS, BONDS, AND REAL PROPERTY

Section Objectives:

- Define stocks.

- Define bonds.

- Describe how a mutual fund distributes investment risk.

- Define real property.

Introduction:

Before we move into some of the standard retirement investment vehicles available to you, we will talk more broadly about stocks, bonds, and real property.

Stocks are shares of a company that infer ownership in the company. One share of stock is one share of ownership. There are two general types of stocks: **common stocks** and **preferred stocks.** Common stocks carry voting rights. Preferred stocks do not carry voting rights, but are guaranteed a certain level of dividend payment before any other stockholders receive dividends. In order for a company to issue stock, the company must become a **publicly traded company**, meaning that its shares are traded on the stock market at places like the New York Stock Exchange or the Chicago Board of Trade. The performance of the stock, which is reflective of how the company performs, on the **stock market** then affects the value of the company. Stock market performance is measured using some key indices, such as the DOW Jones Industrial and NASDAQ in the U.S. There are many indices for different parts of the world, different markets (i.e. technology), etc. The stock market functions on a global scale. Stock market performance in Japan can affect the stock market in the US, Europe, and the rest of Asia. The riskiness of stock investments ranges widely, from low to high risk. The performance of the stock is dependent upon the performance of the company, some of which is under the control of management and some of which is uncontrollable and subject to market pressures, such as supply prices, labor costs, etc.

Money
Matters **101**

Did you know the Chicago Board of Trade is the oldest commodities exchange in the US?

Bonds are a form of debt for the issuer. Governments and companies issue bonds to raise funds for various purposes. Governments issue bonds to finance schools, wars, roads, and other activities. Examples are war bonds and municipal bonds. Companies issue bonds so they can use external

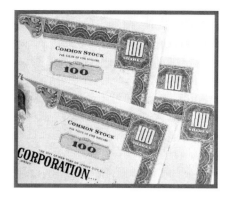

funds to finance long-term projects, such as new buildings or other infrastructure. The language of bonds is slightly different than that of a standard loan. The lender is called the bondholder, or the person who purchases the bond. The issuer is the borrower, who is obligated to repay the bond when it reaches maturity. The coupon is the interest on the loan. Bonds are issued for a specific time frame, typically 10 years or more, when the bond reaches maturity. The issuer sells the bond for less than the face value and guarantees the bondholder payment of the face value of the bond upon maturity. The difference between the face value and the purchase price is the coupon, which reflects the interest earned by the bondholder for loaning the money to the issuer of the bond. Bonds are typically considered a low risk investment, but it is important to understand the risks before purchasing a bond.

> ## Money Matters 102
>
> *Did you know that the first stock tickers and ticker tapes were used in 1867?*

Stocks and bonds are often purchased and managed by **mutual fund** companies. **Mutual funds** are investment tools that can be designed to distribute risk across a number of stocks

and bonds. The idea is that if the portfolio is balanced properly, some investments will increase in value and others will decrease. These changes in value are averaged, and the average change in value is the return for the period. The hope is that the portfolio will either meet or outperform the stock market.

Real property is land and anything that is built on or otherwise attached to it. If your parents own a home, that is considered real property. If you know someone who invests in land or rental properties, those are considered real properties, as well. The term realty is derived from "real property." Real property is typically a fairly stable investment. However, you must be careful of the area in which you make your investment.

House values increased rapidly in many areas of the US at the beginning of the 21st century. This trend stopped quickly in 2007 when the impact of subprime mortgage lending became apparent. Many people borrowed far more money using mortgages with adjustable interest rates than they could afford if the rates increased. The increased demand for homes raised home values because of the basic concept of **supply and demand**, or paying what the market will bear. The market will pay more for a commodity when demand is high than when demand is low. When the interest rates increased, the mortgage payment increased, and made it more difficult or impossible for some of the homeowners with subprime loans to meet their payment obligation. As a result of that, financial institutions began **foreclosing** on homes whose owners were in default on their payments. Foreclosure occurs when a borrower defaults (does not pay) on a loan and the bank takes ownership of the property in lieu of payment. This then led to an increase in the number of houses available for sale (increased supply). In conjunction with the increased number of foreclosures, concerns about a weakening economy reduced the number of people in the home buying market (reduction in demand). As a result, home values increased more slowly or even began to decline. So therefore, if you purchased a high value home when demand was high, you are unlikely to be able to sell it for the purchase cost now that demand for homes has decreased.

Money Matters **103**

Did you know there was a stock exchange in Hawaii from 1910 to 1976?

Stocks, bonds and real property are all assets that should be included in your financial planning and long-term retirement planning. You do need to be careful when making investment decisions. The most effective strategy is to buy low and sell high. This is difficult for many people to understand, because a company stock that is lower than it has been in the past is perceived as a bad investment because the stock has lost value. In fact, this may be a true opportunity. If the company had a setback and is implementing a plan to recover from the setback and continue to grow, it would be a great time to invest because the stock is likely to gain value. The same concept applies to real property. If you find property that seems to be undervalued, perhaps because of location, it may be a great investment opportunity. You need to do your homework before investing, though, to find out the history of the property and any plans for future development in that area.

Concept Reinforcement

1. Define Stocks.

2. Define bonds.

3. Describe how a mutual fund distributes investment risk.

4. Define real property.

SECTION 4.7 –INDIVIDUAL RETIREMENT ACCOUNTS

Section Objectives:

- Define individual retirement accounts.

- List the characteristics of individual retirement accounts.

- Discuss the differences between traditional IRAs and ROTH IRAs.

Introduction:

Individual Retirement Accounts are accounts that are designed for building assets to use during retirement. Individual retirement accounts are also known as IRAs. These accounts provide some significant tax advantages to the person saving for retirement. The first advantage is that the money contributed to the IRA may be contributed pre-tax, or before income and other taxes are paid to the government, depending upon the type of IRA. Roth IRAs are an exception to this idea. The end result of this is that you are taxed on less income than you actually earn, because you have set aside a portion for retirement. A second advantage is that some employers will match what you save, so you end up with double the amount of money you save earning interest toward your retirement. IRAs are accounts you can use to supplement any pension and Social Security income you may have for retirement.

There are several types of IRA accounts: traditional IRAs, ROTH IRAs, SEP IRAs, Simple IRAs, and self-directed IRAs. IRAs, in one form or another, are available to everyone to use as an investment vehicle.

Contributions to traditional IRAs grow tax-free over time and you must pay income tax on the income as you withdraw the funds for retirement. You may begin drawing on funds without penalty at age 59 ½ and are required to begin drawing on the funds at age 70 ½

The second type of IRA is called a Roth IRA. This is a special Roth program to encourage everyone to start saving. The Roth IRA is different than the traditional

Money
Matters **104**

Did you know the maximum Roth IRA contribution limit for 2008 is $5,000?

IRA because contributions are made from earned income (income after tax), so earnings grow tax-free and are not taxed upon withdrawal from the account if you start withdrawals at age 59 ½. A couple more unique qualities are that the IRA owner may, at any time, withdraw up to the total of their contributions (NOT earned interest) without tax or penalty, and up to $10,000 in earning withdrawals are considered qualified (tax free) for those who use the money to purchase a home they will live in. This IRA is named after Senator William Roth of Delaware.

A simplified employee pension (SEP) IRA is a variation on the traditional IRA. Contributions to SEP IRAs are considered part of a profit-sharing plan. The employer may contribute up to 25% of the employee's wages to the employee's SEP IRA account. Contribution limits vary between those who are self-employed and those employed by others. If the employer provides the SEP IRA to one employee, it must be provided to all employees. Calculation of the contribution limits varies between employers and those who are self employed.

The Savings Incentive Match Plan for Employees (SIMPLE) IRA is one type of retirement plan offered by employers. It is a qualified plan, like the 401K and 403B plans, with less administration costs. Contributions to SIMPLE IRAs are made pretax. Employers with less than 100 employees may establish a SIMPLE IRA program and must contribute a minimum amount each year. The employer may either match employee contributions up to 3% of compensation or a flat 2% of compensation for each employee who earns at least $5,000 in the year. This plan also has a catch-up provision for participants who are 50 years old or older.

Self-directed IRAs require the account owner to make investments and investment decisions on behalf of the plan. The IRS requires that a qualified trustee (custodian) hold the IRA assets on behalf of the owner, as well as maintaining all records pertaining to the account. This type of account allows a wide variety of investment options, including real estate, stocks, mortgages, franchises, partnerships, private equity, and tax liens.

> **Money Matters 105**
>
> *Did you know that Albert Einstein said that the greatest miracle known to man is compound interest?*

Investment in IRAs is another area in which a financial planner can help you make decisions about your financial planning. IRAs are one savings tool that you should use, but keep in mind that these are long-term investments and you will be charged a substantial penalty if you withdraw the funds before age 59 ½. If you are making investments with shorter term goals than retirement, there are other appropriate tools, such as mutual funds, money market accounts, and savings accounts.

Concept Reinforcement

1. Define individual retirement accounts.

2. List the characteristics of individual retirement accounts.

3. Discuss the differences between traditional IRAs and ROTH IRAs.

SECTION 4.8 – EMPLOYER-PROVIDED RETIREMENT SAVINGS PLANS

Section Objectives:

- Define 401K and 403B plans.

- List the different types of retirement savings plans.

Introduction:

There are even more ways to save for retirement than we have already discussed. Employers may provide an opportunity for their employees to set aside salary on a tax-deferred basis that will be used for retirement purposes. There are two primary tools used by businesses to provide this benefit: 401k and 403b plans.

The 401k plan is an employer-sponsored defined contribution retirement plan. Why is it called a 401k? Because this plan is described in section 401k of the Internal Revenue Service (IRS) code in the U.S. A defined contribution plan is one that employees contribute to on a voluntary basis and for which the benefits and contributions are not defined by the employer. For example, an employee may choose to maximize her contribution to her 401k plan each year. Another employee may choose not to make any contributions to his 401k plan. The employee decides when and how much to contribute, and the benefit to the employee is based on how well the plan fares in the market.

An employee may choose to defer, or have paid directly into the plan, a specific dollar amount each pay period. This money is paid before the employer calculates state and federal income taxes. The net result is that the person is saving for retirement while reducing the income on which he pays taxes for that year. Taxes are assessed when the employee reaches age 59 ½ and begins to withdraw money from the account. Income taxes are assessed on both the contribution and the interest earned. If the account holder decides to withdraw funds from the plan before age 59 ½, there is an additional 10% tax assessed for early withdrawal. This penalty is a strong incentive to leave 401k contributions in the plan until you are able to withdraw them without incurring the 10% in extra taxes. Another interesting characteristic of a 401k plan

> ## Money Matters 107
>
> *Did you know that beginning in 2007 you can deposit you tax refund directly into your IRA?*

is that most plans allow employees to take loans from the 401k to purchase a home, for example. The loans have to be repaid with interest. The interest paid on the loan is added to the balance of the account as it is paid.

These plans have contribution limits, or a maximum amount of money that can be put in the plan each year. There are provisions for those age 50 and older to make additional "catch-up" payments in addition to the standard maximum limit. These are called the 402g limits, after the section of the IRS code.

Year	Contribution Limit	Catch-up Limit
2007	$15,500	$5,000
2008	$15,500	$5,000
Future years	Not yet determined	

Employers may also contribute to the 401k on behalf of the employee. This is typically done using a matching program in which the employer matches the amount the employee contributes to the plan. There are different maximums for the total contributions (employee + employer). These are set by section 415 of the IRS code and called the 415 limit.

Year	Section 415 Contribution Limit
2006	$44,000
2007	$45,000
2008	$46,000

401k plans typically invest in mutual funds, which may include stocks, bonds, and money market investments. Some employers (publicly traded companies) may offer the option to purchase company stocks. Account owners must start making distributions (taking funds from) the plan at age 70 ½. These are called required minimum distributions.

401k plans are typically offered by companies in the private sector, although an individual who is self employed may establish a 401k. Government agencies and other public (tax funded) employers are not able to provide a 401k plan to their employees.

Money Matters 108

Did you know that the dollar sign is a result of laziness? Instead of writing U.S., it was shortened to S with two vertical lines through it?

A 403b plan is very similar to a 401k plan. The key difference is the type of organization allowed to establish a plan and offer it to employees. The 403b plan is available for public education organizations, 501(c)(3) non-profit organizations (no other type of nonprofit qualifies), and self-employed ministers.

Since both 401k and 403b plans are employer-specific, it is possible to "rollover" a plan from one employer to another so you don't end up with a number of different plans because of a number of changes of employer. You may do the work to rollover the plan yourself or request assistance from a qualified financial planner or accountant.

Concept Reinforcement

1. Define 401K and 403B plans

SECTION 4.9 –REVERSE MORTGAGES

Section Objectives:

- Define reverse mortgage.
- Describe appropriate use of a reverse mortgage in retirement.

Introduction:

We have learned about a number of different ways to save for retirement. For those Americans who own their own homes, the value of the home usually comprises about 60% of the individual's total assets. Remember that an asset is something of value that you own and which can be sold.

A reverse mortgage is available to homeowners age 62 or older in the U.S. A reverse mortgage allows the homeowner to withdraw equity from their homes in the form of a loan (reverse mortgage). The equity can be withdrawn as a lump sum (all at once) or in multiple payments. An interesting point about reverse mortgages is that repayment is not required until the homeowner dies, the house is sold, or the owner leaves the home to go into an assisted living situation or a nursing home. Payments to the homeowner increase the lien (debt) on the house each time a payment is made.

Homes typically increase in value over time, but not always. If the home does increase in value after a reverse mortgage is taken out, there may be an option for the homeowner to take a second reverse mortgage for the increased value of the home.

There are certain requirements for a homeowner to be eligible to opt for a reverse mortgage. The home must be fully paid off, either before the reverse mortgage is taken out, or with the money released with the reverse mortgage. Any remaining funds can be used for any purposes. The borrower must be at least 62 years old and seek free financial counseling from a person or group approved by the US Department of Housing and Urban Development (HUD) to ensure that the borrower and his/her family fully understand what a reverse mortgage is and how to secure one.

Money Matters 110

Did you know the first American motel, named the "Motel Inn," was opened in San Luis Obispo in 1925?

How much money will a reverse mortgage provide to the borrower? There are five primary factors that are taken into consideration when determining this amount:

1. The appraised value of the property, including any repairs that need to be made and any existing liens (money owed) on the house. The higher the appraised value, the more money is likely to be available, depending on pending repairs and existing liens.
2. The interest rate, which is determined by the US Treasury.
3. The age of the borrower. The older the borrower, the more money will be available.
4. The way the payment is taken: a line of credit, lump sum, or monthly payments.
5. The location of the property.

The interest rate on reverse mortgages is adjustable, meaning that it can be adjusted on an annual, semi-annual, or monthly basis, depending upon the program. There are some fixed interest rate programs available for reverse mortgages, but these are the exception.

Most reverse mortgage programs are available through private lending institutions, although there are some low cost reverse mortgage programs available from state and local governments. Remember that the proceeds of reverse mortgages provided by private companies can be used for any purpose by the borrower. This is not true for state and local government programs. The proceeds from these low-cost reverse mortgages must usually be used for specific purposes related to the home itself, such as for home repairs or paying property taxes. The public sector (state and local government) programs are typically quite restrictive in areas where they are available. They are not available in many areas. If they are available, the interest rates are typically lower and there are fewer or no fees incurred with the loan.

The reverse mortgage ends under very specific conditions. The homeowner dies, sells the house, or moves out of the house for 12 consecutive months to receive nursing home care or assisted living. If one of these conditions is met, the home may be either sold or refinanced by the heirs of the homeowner's estate. If the house is sold,

Money
Matters 111

Did you know that Independence Hall is on the back of the $100 bill?

Money
Matters 112

*Did you know that
the rate at which
bills change hands
is called velocity?*

the reverse mortgage will be paid off with the proceeds of the sale. If there is money remaining after the loan is paid off, it goes to the heirs. If the sale of the house brings in less than is owed, the bank absorbs the loss using insurance purchased specifically for that situation.

There are other options for accessing the equity in a senior's home. Examples include home equity lines of credit, some of which require interest-only payments for 10 years. These loans typically have a higher interest rate than the reverse mortgage. These loans typically have fewer up front costs (insurance, etc.) than reverse mortgages. The suitability of each type of loan must be carefully assessed based on the specific situation of the homeowner who wishes to borrow the money.

Concept Reinforcement

1. Define reverse mortgage.

2. Describe appropriate use of a reverse mortgage in retirement.

SECTION 4.10 –OTHER MONEY MANAGEMENT TOPICS

Section Objectives:

- Define phishing.
- List common phishing scams.
- List risks of loaning money to friends or family.

Introduction:

There are some other pitfalls you should look out for when dealing with personal financial management. People are constantly coming up with new "opportunities" they use to separate you from your money. A key example of this is "phishing" on the internet. I'm sure you have heard of the various scams where people send emails saying they have an opportunity for you to earn some money by helping them out.

Some examples include:

Lotteries in foreign countries: The scam is that all you have to do to make a bunch of money is provide your bank account information so the lottery can deposit funds into your account. The only ones who benefit from this are the people to whom you give your information because they will use your personal information for their financial gain.

Moving money from another country: The offer here is that someone in a foreign country has a large amount of money they need your help to move. If you help them move it by allowing them access to your bank account information, they claim that they will give you a significant fee for doing so. Again, this is just a way to get your private financial information.

Official looking emails from financial institutions are often phishing. These organizations will typically contact you by U.S. mail, not email, if they need to confirm or change anything about your accounts with them. If you receive emails like this, contact your financial institution by telephone or in person to figure out whether you have received an official request or not.

> **Money Matters 113**
>
> *Did you know that it is illegal for U.S. currency to bear the portrait of someone who is still living?*

Emails from supposed customers of on-line merchants, such as eBay. People will phish for your private financial information by threatening you regarding a transaction you supposedly made over the web. If this occurs to you, report it immediately to the abuse center for the on-line merchant. It is important that you go to the actual web site of the merchant to report phishing scams. Avoid the links in the email you suspect of being a scam.

These are just a few ways that people try to steal your personal information using the internet. It pays to be extremely cautious when using the internet for financial transactions. Legitimate on-line merchants will have strong security measures in place to prevent phishing, but phishing techniques change quickly, so security software must be updated frequently and cannot be relied on 100% to prevent theft of your personal information. The key point here is to use common sense. If something sounds too good, it probably is not to be trusted.

Wikipedia defines phishing as: "an attempt to criminally and fraudulently acquire sensitive information, such as usernames, passwords, and credit card details, by masquerading as a trustworthy entity in an electronic communication. eBay, PayPal and online banks are common targets. Phishing is typically carried out by email or instant messaging[1] and often directs users to enter details at a website, although phone contact has also been used.[2][2] "Attempts to deal with the growing number of reported phishing incidents include legislation, user training, public awareness, and technical measures."

Another area where you should be cautious in managing your finances is in dealings with family and friends. It is likely at some point that you will be approached by a friend or family member who wants to borrow money, asks you to co-sign a loan, or asks you to help out financially in some other way. Loaning money to friends and family should always be done with the understanding that it may not be paid back to you. If you are not willing to take the financial loss without causing damage to your

1 Tan, Koon. Phishing and Spamming via IM (SPIM). Internet Storm Center. Retrieved on December 5, 2006.

2 Skoudis, Ed. "Phone phishing: The role of VoIP in phishing attacks", searchSecurity, June 13, 2006.

relationship, you should not loan the money. Loaning money to someone on a personal basis is an informal relationship unless you draw up an agreement detailing the repayment terms that both you and the borrower sign. Even then, it could be problematic to recover the money unless you decide to go to court to recover your funds.

Co-signing a loan is another area in which you may be asked for help. It is common for a parent to co-sign a loan for a young adult to help establish a credit rating. An example is to purchase a vehicle. Co-signing helps the person with no credit rating or a poor credit rating get a loan, and possibly better interest rates, than they might be able to get on their own because the credit histories of both parties are considered by the bank. The risk to the person who co-signs the loan is that the person who has agreed to make the payments may default on the payments, leaving the debt with the co-signer.

Money Matters 115

Did you know that the paper used to print bills has a watermark that portrays the same historical figure as the printed portrait?

Concept Reinforcement

1. Define phishing.

2. List common phishing scams.

3. List risks of loaning money to friends or family.

Section **4.6**

Section **4.7**

Section **4.8**

Section **4.9**

Section **4.10**

Additional Notes

Money Management

APPENDIX

MONEY MANAGEMENT ANSWER KEY

MONEY MANAGEMENT UNIT 1

Section 1.1

1. List two types of money that are not official currency.

Answer: Barter, proto money, intermediate commodity.

2. Describe how the barter system works.

Answer: Two parties agree to a trade of goods or services that is mutually beneficial. No money is exchanged in a barter.

3. Describe different types of money.

Answer: Standardized coinage – coins that contain specific weights of precious metals that are agreed to represent a specific value.

Representative money is based on receipts that were given by banks in exchange for deposits of precious metals with the bank. These receipts were traded for goods and services because the holder of the receipt was able to withdraw the value of the deposit that was written on the receipt. This led to the development of paper money that was supported by actual deposits of gold.

Fiat money is similar to representative money, except that it is not backed by actual gold deposits. The value of fiat money is determined by the government and considered legal tender.

Section 1.2

1. Define gross domestic product (GDP).

Answer: Gross domestic product is a measure of the size of an economy. The formula used to calculate gross domestic product is: GDP = consumption + investment + government expenditures + (gross exports - gross imports).

2.   Define economic indicator:

Answer: An economic indicator is a statistic, or measure, about the economy. Economic indicators are used to understand how the economy is performing. These statistics are used to predict how the economy will behave in the future. Unemployment, new jobs, inflation, and gross domestic product are a few of the many statistics used.

3.   Define GDP Per Capita:

Answer: A way to understand how well the economy is doing. This measures the average of how much each individual in a country contributes to the economy of that country. The formula for GDP per capita is:

Gross domestic product (GDP)/population = GDP per capita

For example, a country of 100 people has a GDP of $500,000. The formula for GDP per capita is $500,000/100=$5,000 GDP per capita.

4.   Discuss how personal and national economics affect each other.

Answer: The relationship between personal and national economics is very strong. A healthy economy creates new jobs, which then provide tax revenue to the government. It is important to keep in mind that each job created by business has a broader effect. Each person who has a job buys goods and services, which create other jobs, which make the economy grow. This is called a ripple effect. The same idea applies when jobs are lost. The loss of one job usually leads to the loss of more jobs. Loss of jobs means the economy gets smaller.

Section 1.3

1.   Discuss the importance of personal financial management.

Answer: Personal financial management is important to ensure that you can meet your basic needs of housing, food, transportation and other necessities, as well as saving for future expenses, such as trips and retirement.

2.   Define the concepts of budget, net worth, asset, and liability.

Answer: **Budget: a tool used to manage your money.**

Net worth is the difference between your assets and your liabilities.

Asset is something of monetary value.

Liability is something that is owed.

3.   What is the ultimate goal of personal financial management?

Answer: **Create and live by a budget that allows you to pay essential expenses, pay for loans, save for the future, and give you some discretionary income.**

Section 1.4

1.   List 5 goals of personal money management.

Answer: Any of the following:

Paying bills on time.

Spending less than you earn.

Establishing and maintaining a good credit rating (future chapter).

Using credit cards wisely.

Saving for short-term goals (purchase of a car, for example).

Saving for college.

Saving for a home.

Saving for retirement.

Saving for something special to you (a trip, special purchase).

2.   Describe the difference between saving and investing.

Answer: Saving is a very safe way of building wealth. Money in savings accounts is protected to a certain level by the government. Savings grow at very low interest rates. Investing always involves some risk, but brings the potential of higher returns, thus greater long-term wealth.

3.   List the differences between simple and compound interest.

Simple interest accumulates on the principal. If the money is deposited for multiple years, the interest accumulates only on the amount deposited originally, but not on the interest earned each year.

Compound interest accumulates on both the principal and earned interest. If money is de-

posited for multiple years, the interest is added to the principal each year and the next year's interest is earned based on the previous year's principal + interest.

Section 1.5

1. List two common types of accounts used for personal money management.

Answer: **Checking and savings.**

2. Discuss the pros and cons of on-line banking.

Answer: **Pros – convenience, reduced cost, reduced travel time.**

Cons – potential for hacking and identity theft, phishing, lack of face-to-face contact with a bank employee.

3. List the fees that a bank might impose and how to avoid them.

Answer: **Minimum balance: maintain the minimum required balance in your account(s).**

Overdraft: make sure you have enough money in your account to cover the checks you write. This is one reason to make sure the checking account is balanced on a regular basis.

Stop Payment Fees: be sure that you write checks only to reputable people or businesses.

Service Fee: make sure you avoid the services that incur a fee, such as teller services at some banks.

Checks: choose the least expensive, yet secure, source for your checks.

ATM Fees: be aware of the terms of use for the ATM you use to get money. You will be notified of the fees that you are about to incur. Be aware, too, of your bank's policy on ATM fees.

Section 1.6

1. List key attributes of banks:

Answer: Banks are typically for-profit businesses that act as payment agents for their customers. Bank deposits are insured by the FDIC (Federal Deposit Insurance Corporation) for amounts up to $250,000 per account.

2. List key attributes of credit unions:

Answer: Credit unions are typically non-profit organizations whose owners are the members of the credit union. Anyone who is a member (has an account) has voting rights in how the organization is managed. Credit union deposits are insured only if the members vote to do so. If the membership decides to offer insurance, they have to partner with a private insurance group to provide that insurance.

Section 1.7

1. List the different types of investments.

Answer: Bonds, stocks, certificates of deposit, life insurance, real estate, precious metals.

2. Define investment risk.

Answer: The risk that an investment will lose value. There are several types of investment risk, including currency risk, liquidity risk, financial risk, and market risk. Each applies differently to different types of investments.

Section 1.8

1. Discuss the differences between short and long term investing.

Answer: Short term investing is typically done with a specific short-term goal in mind, such as a down payment for a home or vehicle. Short-term investments often have lower rates of return than long-term investments. Long-term investments are made to have money for retirement or a child's education.

2. Discuss investment strategies.

Answer: Each person has unique financial goals, thus will have a unique investment strategy to meet those goals. An investment strategy typically includes long and short-term investments and should be actively managed.

3. List the two primary goals of socially responsible investing.

Answer: Financial gain and societal good.

4. List 5 goals for financial planning.

Answer: Trip, car, house, education, retirement.

Section 1.9

1. State the recommended percent of income that an individual should save each paycheck.

Answer: 10%

2. Discuss how starting a savings program at a young age affects retirement savings.

Answer: Beginning a savings program at a young age takes advantage of the ability of money to grow over time due to compound interest. The later you start saving, the less time your money has to grow.

Section 1.10

1. List the basic principles in personal budgeting (overview of concept).

Answer: Purpose of budget, simplicity, and flexibility.

2. Discuss allocation percentages as they apply to personal budgeting.

Answer: Allocation percentages are used to develop a budget. For example, no more than 25% of your income should be devoted to rent or mortgage payment. A budget should be based on a reasonable allocation of costs and past spending patterns.

MONEY MANAGEMENT UNIT 2

Section 2.1

1. How does educational level affect earning potential?

Answer: Increased levels of education tend to increase earning potential, with professional degrees (medical, law, etc) providing the most earning potential. Doctorates in other field increase earning potential some what, but have certain limitations due to demand for the skill set and other factors.

2. List costs and benefits of advanced education.

Answer: Advanced education incurs a cost of lost earnings, meaning that the time spent getting an education is not spent earning a salary. It definitely incurs the cost of actually attending school and paying for living expenses. Some of these costs may become long term as the result of student loans, which are repaid over many years.

3. Discuss whether there is a point of diminishing returns in education.

Answer: There may be a point of diminishing returns in education, particularly if you overspecialize in a non-professional field. For example, a doctorate in pottery is not likely to pay as well as a doctorate in biochemistry.

Section 2.2

1. How do people earn money?

Answer: Jobs, self-employment, retirement, investment income.

List how these ways of earning money differ.

2. Answer: Some people have jobs and some don't. Some jobs provide fringe benefits and others don't. For those who do not have fringe benefits, it may be necessary to work a second job to pay for health insurance and save for retirement.

Section 2.3

1. Do you see the relationships between tax rates and filing status in the above table? Describe what you see.

Answer: **Individuals tend to move between tax brackets at lower income amounts. % of tax as income increases enough to change tax brackets.**

2. If a property is worth $25,000 and the mill rate is 15%, calculate the property tax.

Answer: **25000 × .15=$3,750**

Section 2.4

1. Define the essential difference between money earned on a job and through investments.

Answer: **Money earned on the job requires you to perform work. Money earned through investments grows separate from your job.**

2. Define tax-deferred investment and why this is an important savings tool.

Answer: **Tax-deferred investment makes more money available for investment and reduces the investor's tax burden by reducing earned income.**

Section 2.5

1. Compare liquid and non-liquid assets.

Answer: **Liquid assets can be converted to cash easily. An example is the money in a savings account. Non-liquid assets are those that cannot be converted easily to cash.**

2. Define diversification.

Answer: **Diversification is an investment strategy intended to spread investment risk across a number of investments.**

Section 2.6

1. Say why developing and following a budget is important.

Answer: It is important to plan and follow a budget to allow you to provide for your basic necessities of food, shelter, and transportation, as well as to segregate money for savings, trips, and other expenses.

2. List the basic components of a budget (specific components of a budget).

Answer: Gross income, taxes, net income, necessary expenses (housing, food, transportation, utilities, and insurance), and other expenses (savings, entertainment, pets, clothing, and others).

Section 2.7

1. Define a zero sum budget.

Answer: A budget in which debits (outlays) and credits (additions) add up to 0.

2. Discuss why a zero sum budget is important.

Answer: A zero sum budget is important because it results in minimization of debt, as well as ensuring that all of the income is allocated to appropriate categories, including savings and retirement.

Section 2.8

1. Develop a budget based on $2000 in income per month using the concepts in this section.

Answer: The answer will depend upon the values students apply to different variables.

2. Discuss how to track expenses by category.

Answer: Expenses can be tracked by category in a number of ways. The envelope method is an effective way of maintaining receipts by expense category. Expenses may also be tracked using homemade spreadsheets, commercially available software, and paper forms.

Section 2.9

1. Define debit and credit.

Answer: A debit is an outlay from your budget. Debits can reflect expenses, savings, or investment outlays. Credits reflect money that is coming in for you to use. Credits are usually from paychecks, but can also include transfers from other accounts.

2. Describe how to balance your budget.

Answer: Add your debits up. Add your credits up. Subtract your debits from your credits. If you balance is less than zero, you need to reduce your debits. If your balance is greater than zero, you have the opportunity to invest or save additional funds.

Section 2.10

1. Define an emergency fund and discuss the importance of having a financial cushion.

Answer: An emergency fund is a liquid asset, often a savings or money market account, that has enough money to support you and your household for 3-6 months in case of an emergency, such as loss of a job, illness, or a family emergency. This cushion can be critical to your financial health if you are unable to work for some reasons.

2. List some situations in which an emergency fund could prevent financial distress.

Answer: Illness of self or family member, loss of a job, family emergency.

MONEY MANAGEMENT UNIT 3

Section 3.1

1. List types of debt.

Answer: Mortgage loan, car loan, home equity loan, credit card balances, revolving credit accounts.

2. Discuss the difference between positive and negative debt.

Answer: Positive debt results in acquisition of something that has a long-term value that is higher than the cost of the debt. Negative debt does not do this.

Section 3.2

1. Discuss appropriate use of credit cards.

Answer: Credit cards can be used appropriately in a number of ways: to track business and/or personal expenses, to participate in benefit programs, to establish credit.

2. List ways people use credit cards well.

Answer: Travel expenses (if paid off immediately), establishing credit, gaining travel benefits.

3. List ways people use credit cards poorly and end up in financial trouble.

Answer: Purchase things they do not need and/or cannot afford, don't pay off balances and allow interest to build up.

Section 3.3

1. Define checking account and direct deposit.

Answer: A checking account is a transactional account, meaning that the funds in the account are safely deposited in the bank, yet easily available to the account owner. These are also known as demand accounts, because the money is available based on demand generated through check writing, ATM use, etc.

Direct deposit is an electronic transaction between your employer and your bank, in which your paycheck is electronically deposited in your checking account (or whatever account you designate) on your regular payday.

2. List the four primary tools used to withdraw funds from a checking account.

Answer: The primary tools used to access the funds in a checking account are checks, debit cards, direct debits, and automated teller machine (ATM) transactions.

3. List characteristics of debit cards and their appropriate use.

Answer: Debit cards are plastic cards, which look like credit cards. When the user makes a transaction using a debit card, the funds are withdrawn directly from the checking account associated with the debit card. It is very important to track debit card transactions the same way you track other withdrawals from your checking account to make sure that you stay out of an overdraft situation. It is also very important to protect your debit card from theft because the transactions made with it withdraw funds directly from your checking account. If someone else gets your debit card and uses it, those funds are not available to you.

4.   Describe how to balance a checking account.

Answer: Beginning balance + credits –debits – pending debits.

Section 3.4

1.   Define credit score.

Answer: A credit score is the result of statistical analysis of your financial habits, and thus your creditworthiness. Creditworthiness is an assessment of how likely a person is to pay bills on time. Credit scores fall in a range of 300 to 850, with 850 being the best possible credit rating. Most people fall in the range of 650 and 799.

2.   Name the three primary consumer credit bureaus in the US.

Answer: Experion, Equifax, and TransUnion.

3.   Discuss how a consumer can use these agencies to maintain a healthy credit score.

Answer: Obtain annual credit reports; monitor accounts and request investigations of suspicious accounts.

Section 3.5

1. List financial actions that have positive and negative impact on credit scores.

Answer: Positive behaviors: paying bills on time, monitoring your credit report and correcting any errors you find, carefully managing the number of credit cards and other loans in your name, as well as the number of "hard" credit checks by institutions to which you apply for credit, and generally living within your means (spending less than you earn).

Negative behaviors: paying bills late, defaulting on bills or loans, applying for too many lines of credit or loans, and living beyond your means (spending more than you earn).

2. Define FICO score and list the 5 primary types of information used to calculate the FICO score.

Answer: FICO is the most widely used method to determine credit score. Payment history, amount owed, length of credit history, new credit, and types of credit used.

Section 3.6

1. Discuss how credit scores impact a person's ability to receive loans.

Answer: The higher a credit score, the lower the risk to the bank of loaning money.

2. Discuss how credit scores impact interest rates.

Answer: People with higher credit scores are likely to get lower interest rates, or prime + ?%, than those with low credit scores.

Section 3.7

1. Define identity theft.

Answer: Identity theft is a term for crimes that occur when one person illegally uses another person's identity for some purpose. Identity theft is typically divided into four types: financial, criminal, identity cloning, and business/commercial identity theft.

2. Discuss how to avoid identity theft.

Answer: Monitor credit report, protect personal information, leave your Social Security Card and number at home, shred financial statements and credit card offers before disposal, protect your wallet, and report lost or stolen cards immediately to both the police and the credit card company.

Section 3.8

1. Define a collection agency.

Answer: A collection agency is a business that attempts to collect debts owed by individuals or businesses. The collections agency is typically paid a percent of the debt recovered as a commission.

2. Discuss the process of debt going to collections agencies.

Answer: Lawsuit filed by lender, response to lawsuit, obtain default judgment, collect money through sale of property, belonging, receipt of payment, etc.

3. Discuss how to work with a collection agency to resolve problems.

Answer: Work with the collection agency to work out payment terms that all parties can accept, then be sure to meet your payment obligations.

Section 3.9

1. Define bankruptcy.

Answer: Bankruptcy is a legal status that declares the inability, or impairment of the ability, of a person or business to pay debts (pay their creditors).

2. Discuss how to avoid bankruptcy.

Answer: Live within your means, follow a budget, and deal with problems immediately.

3. Discuss the impact of bankruptcy on credit rating.

Answer: You will not be able to get a loan for seven years, then pay higher rates until you re-establish your good credit.

Section 3.10

1. Discuss how to get out of negative debt.

Answer: Sell assets, take a second job, reduce spending.

MONEY MANAGEMENT UNIT 4

Section 4.1

1. Define long term financial planning.

Answer: It is engaging in an active process of managing your income and assets to allow you to retire in the lifestyle in which you have become accustomed to living, or however you define a retirement lifestyle.

2. Discuss the importance of long term financial planning.

Answer: It means that you are able to save and invest enough money while you are working to allow you to have a comfortable retirement where you will not have to worry too much about money.

3. What is the rule of 72?

Answer: The rule of 72 is a method for estimating doubling time of an investment in years, based on compound interest. The formula is 72/interest rate = time to doubling.

Section 4.2

1. List 3 ways to pay for college.

Answer: 529 plans, scholarships/grants, loans, work-study, and graduate assistantships.

2   Discuss how each can affect long-term financial stability of the student.

Answer: 529 plans, scholarships, grants, work-study and graduate assistantships all provide the student money for education that does not have to be paid back. When the student enters the workforce, she does so without debt from these financial sources. Scholarships and grants may carry other obligations, such as working for the funding organization for a certain time, but this is not common. Student loans accumulate while the student is in school and must be repaid after graduation. The long-term impact to the student is that he must include the loan repayment in his budget for the next 20 years, on average, which reduces the funds available for other purposes such as investing for retirement or saving for a home.

Section 4.3

1.   List considerations when purchasing a vehicle.

Answer: Cost, purpose, available funds and reason

2.   Discuss the differences between lease and purchase.

Answer: A lease costs less in the short term, but you do not own the car. Purchasing costs more in the short term, but you own the car.

3.   Discuss when leases are appropriate

Answer: If you want to have more car than you can afford to buy, trade cars frequently, and don't drive a lot of miles.

4.   Discuss when purchase is appropriate.

Answer: If you want to own the car, and if you drive a lot of miles.

5.   List considerations in buying a new vehicle vs. a used vehicle.

Answer: New vehicle – warranty, no history of use, and choose the options you want. Used vehicle – lower cost, no loss of value when you drive off the lot, and someone else may have owned it – you don't know its full history.

Section 4.4

1.   Discuss how saving for a home purchase can reduce overall home purchase costs.

Answer: If you save 20%, you will not pay mortgage insurance. The more you save for a down payment, the less you will have to repay, therefore the less interest you will pay.

2.   Name 3 key considerations in determining how much home one can afford.

Answer: Income, living expenses, and debt.

3.   Discuss research the homebuyer should do to understand the real cost of owning a home.

Answer: Utility costs, tax costs, and upgrades.

Section 4.5

1.   Discuss the importance of retirement planning.

Answer: It is important to plan for retirement so you have enough money to live the lifestyle you want to live, in addition to meeting your basic needs of food, shelter, and health care.

2.   List issues that need to be considered in retirement planning.

Answer: Retirement benefits accrued at each job, IRA/403B income, Social Security income, lifestyle, basic cost of living, and health care costs.

Section 4.6

1.   Define Stocks.

Answer: Stocks are shares of ownership in a publicly traded company.

2.   Define bonds.

Answer: Bonds are loans to the government that have a guaranteed interest rate and can be redeemed for the dollar amount of the bond after the bond has matured.

3.   Describe how a mutual fund distributes investment risk.

Answer: A mutual fund distributes investment risk by diversifying investments across a number of investment types.

4. Define real property.

Answer: Real property is land or anything that is built on or attached to it.

Section 4.7

1. Define individual retirement accounts.

Answer: IRAs are accounts designed to build assets for retirement.

2. List the characteristics of individual retirement accounts.

Answer: Contributions to traditional IRAs grow tax-free over time. The earliest age of distribution is 59 ½. Required distributions begin at 70 ½. There are annual contribution limits.

3. Discuss the differences between traditional IRAs and ROTH IRAs.

Answer: Traditional IRAs are funded pre-tax and Roth IRAs are funded post-tax.

Section 4.8

1. Define 401K and 403B plans

Answer: A 401K is an employer-sponsored defined contribution retirement plan. The 403b plan an employer-sponsored defined contribution retirement plan that is available for public education organizations, 501(c)(3) non-profit organizations (no other type of nonprofit qualifies), and self-employed ministers.

Section 4.9

1. Define reverse mortgage.

Answer: A reverse mortgage allows the homeowner to withdraw equity from their homes in the form of a loan.

2. Describe appropriate use of a reverse mortgage in retirement.

Answer: Appropriate use includes maintenance of the home and living expenses. The proceeds from low-cost publicly funded reverse mortgages must usually be used for specific purposes related to the home itself, such as for home repairs or paying property taxes.

Section 4.10

1. Define phishing.

Answer: Phishing is a way that people try to get your personal financial information over the internet.

2. List common phishing scams.

Answer: Lotteries in other countries, requests for help transferring money, official looking emails from financial institutions, and emails from supposed customers of on-line retailers.

3. List risks of loaning money to friends or family.

Answer: You may not be repaid, the possibility of ruining relationships, and co-signing loans could result in additional debt.

INDEX: